Piazza San Marco
and Its Museums

Eugenia Bianchi
Nadia Righi
Maria Cristina Terzaghi

Piazza San Marco and Its Museums

Electa

Cover
Francesco Guardi, *Piazza San Marco
with the Basilica and the Clock Tower*, detail.
Edinburgh, National Gallery of Scotland.

Translation
Richard Sadleir

Contents

Piazza San Marco

Admired by Petrarch in the 14th century, described by Napoleon as the "finest drawing-room in the world," Piazza San Marco is the undisputed symbol of Venice. Once the centre of the political, religious and cultural life of the Venetian Republic, now it is one of the most famous tourist sights in the world. The focus of St. Mark's basin, with its 12,000 square metres of surface area, it is the only square to be called a "piazza" in the whole of Venice, with its urban fabric composed of courts of various sizes known as "campi" and "campielli." Gazing across this splendid and busy "drawing-room," on which stand some of the most significant buildings in the city's centuries of history, it is difficult to imagine that it once was a field traversed by a stream called the *Batario*, on the sides of which stood the churches of San Geminiano and San Teodoro. By the second half of the 12th century the square, named after St. Mark when the first basilica was built (832), had begun to acquire its present appearance. Under the Doge Sebastiano Ziani it was decided to demolish San Geminiano (later rebuilt by Sansovino in the 16th century on the spot now occupied by the Ala Napoleonica or Napoleonic Wing), and the old battlemented walls that used to encircle the square were partly replaced by buildings with porticoes and loggias.

In 1264 it was paved with brick, and then repaved in 1722 by Andrea Tirali with flagstones of trachyte, and other buildings were gradually erected. Today Piazza San Marco is a large trapezium-shaped space, bounded on the east by the Basilica of San Marco, on the north by the Procuratie Vecchie with their Clock Tower, on the south by the Procuratie Nuove and on the west by the Ala Napoleonica. On the south-west corner stands, in isolation, the bell-tower, beyond which one enters in the smaller Piazzetta di San Marco, enclosed between the Doge's Palace and the Libreria Sansoviniana, while to the left of the basilica is the Piazzetta dei Leoni, named for its two marble statues of *lions* of the 18th century.

When the **bell-tower of San Marco** collapsed on 14 July 1902, the square lost its oldest monument after the basilica: begun under the Doge Pietro Tribuno (888–912) it was completed in the third quarter of the 12th century. Frequently restored, it was restructured between 1511 and 1514 to a design by Giorgio Spavento, with a taller belfry and a cusp surmounted by a statue of the *Archangel Gabriel*. After its collapse, the tower was rebuilt (1903–1914) "as it was, where it was." Almost 100 metres tall, it consists of a brick shaft with a cross-section twelve metres square. This is decorated with pilasters

The Clock Tower, detail.

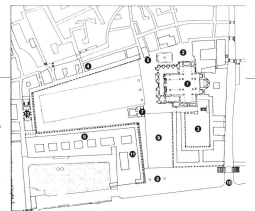

Plan of Piazza San Marco.
1. Basilica of San Marco
2. Piazzetta dei Leoni
3. Doge's Palace
4. Procuratie Vecchie
5. Clock Tower
6. Procuratie Nuove
7. Campanile of SanMarco

8. Columns with the Lion of St. Mark and St. Theodore
9. Piazzetta San Marco
10. Ponte della Paglia
11. Libreria Sansoviniana
12. Ala Napoleonica

and a row of round-headed windows. The belfry, made of Istrian stone, is surmounted by a balustrade and a dado decorated with reliefs of *Justice* and the *Lion of St. Mark*. On the pyramidal cusp, sheathed in copper, stands the gilded figure of an *Angel*, a copy by L. Zandomeneghi (1822) of the Cinquecento original. Access to the bell-tower is by lift or a spiral staircase with thirty-six flights of steps (entry in the Loggetta): from the top one gets a splendid view over Venice.

Adjoining the east side of the bell-tower is the **Loggetta di San Marco**, also destroyed in 1902 and immediately rebuilt using the original fragments. Designed by Jacopo Sansovino (between 1537 and 1549) it is slightly raised above the piazza level: the structure consists of round-headed arches flanked by coupled columns of a composite order. Below are niches containing bronze statues of *Minerva*, *Mercury*, *Apollo*, and *Peace*, carved by Sansovino in 1540–1545. The front of the attic, above the arches, is decorated by rectangular panels with reliefs of the *Isle of Candia*, *Venice as Justice*, and the *Isle of Cyprus*, by followers of Sansovino (Tiziano Minio, Danese Cattaneo and Gerolamo Lombardo), while the *Cupids* in the other panels are 18th-century work. The marble balustrade, similar to that at the base, dates from the mid-17th century. The imposing

Overhead view of the five domes of the Basilica of San Marco.

Piazza San Marco.

The **Caffè Florian**, under the arcading of the Procuratie Nuove, is one of the most celebrated locations in Venice. Its patrons have included Casanova, Goldoni, Parini, Byron, Foscolo, Goethe, Rousseau and many others.

It was founded in 1720 by Floriano Francesconi, who named it the "Caffè Venezia Trionfante," and was completely restructured in the mid-19th century.

bronze gate was made by Antonio Gai in 1735–1737. In a niche in the end wall of the interior there is a terracotta group of the *Madonna and Child and St. John the Baptist* by Sansovino.

On the side opposite the bell-tower, the **Procuratie Vecchie** extend for about 150 metres. Now used as offices, they were originally the residences of the *procurators* or overseers of San Marco, entrusted with the maintenance of and improvements to the basilica. Begun by Mauro Codussi before 1500 on the site of a 12th-century structure, the building was completed in 1514–1532 by Bartolomeo Bon il Giovane and Guglielmo Dei Grigi, with some parts by Sansovino. The building has three orders of round-headed arches opening below into an arcade, and ends to the east in the **Clock Tower**, also probably designed by Mauro Codussi in 1496–1499 and flanked in the early Cinquecento by two rectangular buildings redesigned c. 1755 by Giorgio Massari. The tower rises above a broad arch and consists of three orders bounded by pilasters and trabeations. On the first floor there is an enamelled and gilded clock made by Paolo and Giovanni Carlo Re-

Gentile Bellini,
Translation of the Relics
of the Cross, *Venice,*
Gallerie dell'Accademia.

The **Translation of the Relics of the Cross**, executed by Gentile Bellini in 1496 to commemorate the transfer of the relics of the Cross to the Scuola di San Giovanni Evangelista, depicts Piazza San Marco. The original frescoes can be seen in the facade of the Basilica of San Marco. To the left are the Procuratie Vecchie before construction of the Clock Tower and to the right the Hospice of Sant'Ursula, demolished in the 16th century.

nieri da Reggio in 1499; it shows the hours and the phases of the moon and zodiac. On the second storey there is an aedicule containing a bronze *Madonna and Child* flanked by two windows showing the hours, while on the third storey stands a carving of the *Lion of St. Mark*. In the attic storey are the famous **Moors**, two bronze statues cast by Ambrogio delle Ancore in 1497. They represent a youth and a bearded man who strike the hours with hammers on a bell.

Opposite the Procuratie Vecchie range the **Procuratie Nuove**, designed by Vincenzo

Canaletto,
The Piazzetta, *1727.*
London, Royal
Collection.

Canaletto, Piazza
San Marco viewed
from the Clock Tower.
New York, Private
Collection.

*View of the Piazzetta
of San Marco with
the Doge's Palace
facing the basin.*

In the late 17th century the custom of doing the **"Grand Tour"** spread, especially among youthful members of the English nobility. Generally accompanied by a tutor, they would travel through the leading European countries, visiting Italy in particular and above all Venice, which afforded a free and brilliant social life. Visits would often be timed to coincide with Carnival, when the "tourist" could mingle with the crowd and take part freely in all the

Scamozzi in 1584 on the model of the adjoining Libreria Sansoviniana. Construction had reached the tenth arch when the architect died (1616) and the building was completed c. 1640 by Baldassarre Longhena. The three orders of arches are flanked by pillars, with an imposing range of Doric columns (below), Ionic (centre) and Corinthian (above). On the third level the arches contain rectangular windows surmounted by a tympanum and partly enriched in the later Cinquecento with sculpture by Girolamo Campagna, Tiziano Aspetti and Virgilio Rubino.

The west side of the square is screened off by the structure known as the **Ala Napoleonica**, erected c. 1810 on a site previously occupied by Sansovino's church of San Geminiano. It is by Giuseppe Maria Soli and Giovanni Antolini and has two orders of arches, similar to those of the Procuratie Nuove, surmounted by a tall attic storey topped by statues of Roman emperors and gods. Inside a monumental staircase leads to the Neo-Classical *Salone Napoleonico*, decorated by Giuseppe Borsato in 1822. The present structure houses the *Museo Civico Correr*, a muncipal collection.

pleasures, observing the entertainments that were mounted in the streets. Before leaving he might well commission a view of Venice to take home as a memorial of his visit. The most famous and sought-after were the views painted by Canaletto (1697–1768), who was unmatched in his skilful depictions of city scenes, which are still evocative images of Venice.

Detail of the decorations of the Clock Tower.

The Basilica of San Marco

This is the religious monument most representative of Venice and one of the most original works of mediaeval architecture existing in Italy.

Erected in the 9th century as the Doge's chapel (it was only made a cathedral in 1807) and to enshrine the relics of St. Mark, smuggled out of Alexandria in 828 by the merchants Rustico da Torcello and Buono di Malamocco, it stands on the former site of the church of San Teodoro, the earlier patron saint of Venice. The first basilica dedicated to St. Mark was erected in 829–832 in the form of a Latin cross with three naves, apsed presbytery, crypt and narthex. After its destruction in 976 during a popular rebellion against the Doge Pietro Candiano IV, in 978 a second church was built, probably similar to the first. Finally in 1063, under Doge Domenico Contarini (1043–1070), it was decided to build a third basilica, one worthy of the splendour of the Serenissima Repubblica.

In 1094, when it was consecrated, the structure was already complete, while decoration and restoration work (by Sansovino, for instance) continued steadily through the centuries. The plan of the basilica was probably devised by a Greek architect assisted by Venetian and Lombard workmen. The organisation and mosaics are inspired by Oriental models, such as the churches of Hagia Sophia and the Holy Apostles in Constantinople. The plan follows the Greek cruciform arrangement (but with the cross-arm foreshortened), and is surmounted by five slightly elliptical cupolas, resting on barrel vaults raised on sturdy pillars. Each arm, except that of the presbytery, is flanked by two aisles bounded by marble columns and vaulted arches, with cupolas above the pillars of the middle arm. Above runs a gallery (originally the *matroneum*), with access from the atrium by a door to the left of the main porch.

The interior receives light from a series of windows in the base of the cupolas and in the apse, as well as from lunettes in the side walls. This structure is masked by the **facade**, with its two architectural orders defined by five arches, the middle two being the largest. The two levels are separated by a terrace (access from the atrium) at the centre of which, in front of a large window, is a gilded copy of a *Quadriga* (the original is now in the collection of the Museum of San Marco), which had been sent to Venice from Constantinople by Doge Enrico Dandolo at the time of the Fourth Crusade (1204).

Mosaic of the "Archway of the Passion" depicting Christ crucified, detail.

Plan of the Basilica of San Marco as it is today.

The arches of the lower level, taller and set slightly forward compared to those above, are separated by pillars surrounded by a double row of marble columns with fine capitals of Eastern workmanship. Above them are six Byzantine *bas-reliefs* from the 12th century representing (from left) *Hercules and the Erymanthian Boar*, the *Madonna*, *St. George*, *St. Demetrius*, the *Archangel Gabriel* and *Hercules and the Ceryneian Hind*. Each arch with its porch presents a dense cluster of projecting minor arches, statuettes and reliefs that create, together with the mosaics in the lunettes, a particularly effective interplay of light and shade, especially at certain times of day. The oldest *porch*, from the basilica of 978, is the one on the left named after St. Alipio. It has an architrave with reliefs of New Testament subjects (the *Miracle of Cana*, *Epiphany*, the *Annunciation to the Shepherds*, *Christ and the Apostles*) and an inflected arch surmounted by two *Prophets* on a gold ground and containing reliefs of the *Symbols of the Evangelists*. In the lunette of the arch is the *Translation of the Body of St. Mark*, the oldest mosaic in the facade (1260–1270): it is also of interest because

it documents the appearance of the basilica in the 13th century. The next porch has bronze 14th-century doors bearing the signature of one Bertuccio, a Venetian goldsmith. It consists of an arch containing a Gothic triforium and decorated with an early 13th-century relief of *Christ with Two Prophets*. The mosaic in the spherical vault dates from 1728 and depicts *St. Mark Venerated by a Doge*, designed to a cartoon by Sebastiano Ricci. The middle arch is the most monumental and is decorated with outstanding carvings. The arches that follow the profile of the lunette have splendid Romanesque 12th-century reliefs depicting the *Earth*, *Ocean*, *Animal Patterns* and *Crafts* (lower arch); and the *Months*, *Virtues* and *Beatitudes* (upper arch). The band marking the profile of the vault is decorated with natural motifs (in the extrados) and *Crafts* and *Christ with the Prophets* (in the intrados). The last figure on the left (with crutches) is said to

Facade of the Basilica of San Marco.

The Quadriga from Constantinople, full view and detail. Museum of San Marco.

Portal of Sant'Alipio in
the facade of San Marco.

Mosaic on the lunette
above the Portal
of Sant'Alipio.

The **Translation
of the Body of St. Mark
to the Basilica** on the
lunette above the Portal
of Sant' Alipio is the only
ancient mosaic preserved
on the facade (c. 1260). It
shows the Basilica of San
Marco as it must have
looked in the mid-13th century,
before the Gothic
sculptural decorations
were added, with the
middle window framed
by arches and transennae
and with a smaller
number of columns
in the lower order.
Clearly visible are the four bronze horses on
the second-storey
terrace.

Relief on the main arch of the facade depicting the "Squeraroli" (shipwrights).

One of the reliefs on the intrados of the middle arch depicting the month of February.

Figure of a Virtue in the extrados of the second archway of the main Portal of San Marco.

arches, enriched with cusps, aedicules and statues. Among the most interesting examples of Gothic sculpture in Italy, this ornamental complex was begun in 1384 by Pier Paolo and Iacobello Dalle Masegne but mostly executed in the early 15th century by Lombard and Florentine workmen. The sculptors included Matteo Raverti, who probably executed the four *mouldings* at the springing line of the arches, and Piero and Niccolò Lamberti: the former executed the fine *reliefs* on the central arch with *Stories of Genesis, Prophets, Evangelists* and *Fathers of the Church*; the latter some of the s*tatues*, including *St. Mark* and the *angels* in the central cusp.

represent the architect of St. Mark's angrily biting a finger after his dismissal by the Procurators. Tradition holds that he was punished for having boasted, after completing the basilica, that he could build a better one. The mosaic in the vault dates from 1836 and replaces a lost 12th-century original, while the bronzework on the doors of the porch are original 6th-century work. The porch of the fourth arch is similar to the second one, with a mosaic of *St. Mark's Body Welcomed by the Venetians*, composed in about 1660 to a cartoon by Pietro della Vecchia. This artist also designed the *Translation of the Body of St. Mark* in the next arch, altered into a window when the Zen chapel was built. On the architrave is an ancient bas-relief of *Christ Blessing*, perhaps from the basilica of 978.

The arches on the upper level contain mosaics from 1617–1618 after cartoons by Maffeo da Verona (from the left the *Deposition, Descent to Limbo, Resurrection, Ascension*). The arches are crowned by a rich *pediment* of inflected

Door with a Byzantine arch above the Zen chapel.

St. Mark Blessing, a statue in the central arch of the west facade.

Prophet. First arch of the west facade.

The **side elevations** of the basilica, also defined by two orders of arches divided by a terrace, repeat the architectural scheme of the facade and are decorated with sculptures, marbles and mosaics dating from the 12th and 14th centuries. On the west side, towards the Doge's Palace, in the second arch there opens the door of the Baptistry (14th century), in front of which stand the two *Pilastri Acritani*, so called because they come from the church of St. John in Acre, from which they were removed after the victory against the Genoans in 1256, under Lorenzo Tiepolo. Interesting specimens of 6th century Syrian art, they consist of a shaft with a square section decorated with vines, plant volutes, and monogrammes; the capitals have the form of a truncated pyramid inverted. On the outer wall of **St. Mark's Treasury** stands the admirable group of the *Tetrarchs*, a Syrian or Egyptian sculpture from the 4th century AD, and a series of marble *plutei* and decorated bas-reliefs from the 9th–11th centuries.

Passing to the north side, towards the Piazzetta dei Leoni, there is the *Porta dei Fiori*, surmounted by an inflected arch and decorated with sculptures, including a Romanesque

Nativity Scene from the 13th century. Note also the rich sculptural decoration on the upper storey, with statues of *Patriarchs* and *Virtues* by Niccolò Lamberti and interesting *mouldings*, probably by Lamberti's son Piero.

Passing through the main porch, one enters the **atrium** or **narthex**, decorated throughout with marbles and splendid mosaics. The paving is *opus sectile*, laid with marble tiles of differing shapes and arranged in large circles. It dates from the 11th–12th centuries, while the mosaics in the vaults, mostly dealing with *Old Testament Scenes*, were executed in the course of the 13th century. Starting from the right-hand bay, one finds the *Door of St. Clement*, with 11th-century bronzework from

The porphyry group of Tetrarchs *on plinth of the Treasury.*

Marble panels carved in Constantinople and Venice, embedded in the Treasury facade (11th and 12th centuries).

The elegant "Portal of Flowers" on the north side of the Basilica of San Marco.

The **Tetrarchs**, also called The Moors, represent two pairs of warriors embracing; most likely they are the Emperors Diocletian and Maximian, Valerian and Constans. A popular legend holds that these figures are four Saracens who were turned to stone when trying to steal the Cathedral treasure.

The cupola of Genesis in the narthex.

View of the interior of San Marco towards the presbytery.

Constantinople, flanked by powerful coupled columns with fine capitals carved with the heads of lions and eagles. The cupola, called the *Genesis cupola*, is sheathed in fine mosaics from the early 13th century, ranged on three levels and depicting episodes of the Book of Genesis, from the *Creation of the Heavens and Earth* to the *Expulsion from Eden*. On the spandrels and lunettes are figures of *cherubim* and *Stories of Cain and Abel*. The singular energy and strongly naturalistic and descriptive force of the these works are typical of Romanesque art in Northern Italy.

A similar style is carried on into the mosaics in the next arch on the left, with *Stories of Noah* and *The Flood*. Those in the niches of the following bay reveal the strong influence of Ravenna: they depict the *Madonna and Saints*, and the *Apostles*, dating from the early 12th century.

The mosaics of the vault above and on the walls, including *St. Mark in Ecstasy*, are Cinquecento works based on cartoons by Tit-

Detail of a marble column in the interior of the basilica.

Examples of the splendid classical and Byzantine capitals on columns dividing the aisles.

ian and Pordenone. In the same bay note the red marble paving slab set in the pavement opposite the entrance, where according to tradition Pope Alexander III and Frederick Barbarossa met in 1177.

The mosaics of the cupola in the third bay and those in the adjoining arches date from the early decades of the 13th century. The former represent *Episodes from the Bible* and the latter *St. Alipio and St. Simon, Justice*, and *Stories of Abraham* and the *Prophets*. In the fourth bay, which rests like the following one on a broad exedra, is the *tomb of the Doge Bartolomeo Gradenigo*, a Pisan sculpture from the mid-14th century, while the cupola and spandrels are covered with mosaics of *Stories of St. Joseph Hebrew* and *Prophets*, dating from the early 13th century but partly relaid in the 19th.

Much of the mosaic decoration of the last atri-

um has also been restored: the original sections include the *Stories of St. Joseph* and the *Evangelists* of the sixth bay. Finally, in the exedra of the fifth bay, there is the *Sarcophagus of the Doge Marino Morosini*, from the middle of the 13th century: its slab, carved in relief, is more ancient still.

Through the *Arch of Paradise* of the atrium, decorated with mosaics after cartoons by Tintoretto, one enters the solemn **interior**. It is richly decorated with mosaics on a gold ground which cover all the upper surfaces and have a twofold purpose, sacred and civic: to exalt the Church of Christ and celebrate the Venetian church and state.

The decoration, begun in 1072 under Doge Domenico Selvo (1071–1085), continued with restoration work, redecoration and extensions down to the late-19th century. It thus combines a wide range of different styles in an overall

Interior of the Basilica of San Marco, with the galleries above the side-aisles of the middle arm of the church.

harmony created by the richness of the decoration and the splendid gilding.

Going through the Arch of the Apocalypse, also covered in Cinquecento mosaics, one passes under the dome known as the cupola of Pentecost, splendid with mosaics in Byzantine style from the mid-12th century; they depict the *Holy Spirit* surrounded by *Representatives of the Peoples Converted by the Apostles* and *Angels* in the spandrels. The *Arch of the Passion* follows, with early 13th-century mosaics illustrating, with typical Romanesque expressiveness, episodes from the *Passion of Christ* and, immediately after, the *cupola of the Ascension*, with fine mosaics from the early 13th century depicting the *Ascension of Christ within a Circle Borne by Angels, Mary among Angels and the Apostles* and, between the simple windows below and on the spandrels, *Virtues, Evangelists* and *Biblical Rivers*. Byzantine in-

fluences mingle with reminiscences of Northern Romanesque in the mosaics (early-13th century) on the underside of the first arch of the right transept. They depict *Christ Washing the Disciples' Feet*, the *Last Supper*, the *Temptations of Christ* and *Christ's Entry into Jerusalem*. Also from the 13th century is the mosaic decoration of the nearby *Cupola of St. Leonard* or *of the Holy Sacrament*, completed in the spandrels and soffits of the arches with 14th- and 15th-century work. The vault of the main chapel has mosaics from various centuries. From the later decades of the 16th century and early 17th date the *Epiphany, Annunciation, Resurrection, Presentation at the Temple* and *Baptism* on the soffit of the first arch, partly after cartoons by Tintoretto, while the mosaics in the cupola are from the late 12th and 13th century: they represent *Christ Surrounded by the Madonna and Prophets*. The

Christ in the dome of the apse is an early Cinquecento *rifacimento*.

The left transept is also decorated with mosaics. Those on the soffit of the first arch were executed to cartoons by Tintoretto, Giuseppe Salviati and Veronese. The cupola is named after *St. John the Baptist*, and was decorated with mosaics of the Veneto-Byzantine period from the early 13th century depicting *Stories of St. John the Baptist*, while the great *Genealogical Tree of Maria* on the end wall was executed by Antonio Bianchini to a cartoon by Salviati (1542–1551). The New Testament episodes on the arch above are from the late 13th century.

We now return to the main entrance of the basilica. At the start of the **right nave** are two interesting bas-reliefs, a *Madonna Praying* (above the porch of St. Clement) and a *Christ between the Madonna and St. John the Baptist*, both works of the 12th century Byzantine school.

Note, further on, some remains of the original

The cupola of the Ascension.

Christ washes the disciples' feet. A 13th-century mosaic in the "Archway of the Passion."

Mosaic of the Jesse Tree by Antonio Bianchini. Left transept, end wall.

paving with *doves and vegetable motifs.* On the right is the door of the **Baptistry**, a large chapel built under Doge Andrea Dandolo (1343–1354) that screens off the south side of the narthex. It is divided into three communicating spaces, surmounted by cupolas decorated with mosaics. The *baptismal font* in the centre was designed in 1545 by Jacopo Sansovino, who also designed the cover, and was executed by Tiziano Minio da Padova and Desiderio di Firenze. Completed only in 1565, it has a monolithic basin in Egyptian syenite and is enclosed by a sheet of bronze divided into eight panels depicting the *Evangelists* and *Stories of St. John the Baptist.* The statue of *St. John the Baptist* on the apex is by Francesco Segala (1575).

By the entrance is the Gothic *Tomb of the Doge Giovanni Soranzo* (c. 1328), opposite which stands the *Sarcophagus of Andrea Dandolo* (1354), among the most richly decorated funerary monuments in the basilica, by some scholars attributed to Andriolo De Sanctis. Set against one wall of the anti-Baptistry is the *Tombstone of Jacopo Sansovino.*

The altar rests on a block of granite on which tradition has it Christ once stood to preach to the crowds. It was probably brought to Venice by the Doge Domenico Michiel in 1126. Coeval with the erection of the Baptistry are the mosaics in the cupolas and vaults by artists trained in the Byzantine tradition but also versed in Venetian painting at the height of the 14th century.

In the first cupola is *Christ in Glory Surrounded by the Nine Celestial Orders*; in the second *Christ Orders the Apostles to Baptise*, and the *Apostles Baptising*; in the third a *head*

marked with a cross shines on eight Prophets. Also note the mosaics on the walls of the first and second bay illustrating *Stories of St. John the Baptist.*

On the opposite side of the altar is the door giving entry to the **Zen chapel**, added in the 16th century as the funerary chapel of Cardinal Giovanni Battista Zen, whose sepulchre stands in the middle of the chamber. The monument was carved by the sculptor and mason Paolo Savin at the start of the Cinquecento. It consists of a sheet of bronze with the figure of the

Mosaic in the Baptistry depicting Salome's Dance.

The Arc of Andrea Dandolo *in the Baptistry, attributed by some scholars to Andriolo De Sanctis and by others to a follower.*

Interior of the Baptistry with the font by Jacopo Sansovino.

cardinal richly adorned and surrounded by coats of arms and a series of *Virtues*. On the altar between *St. Peter* and *St. John the Baptist*, also by Savin, is a *Madonna and Child*, a fine bronze statue by Antonio Lombardo (c. 1515), known as the *Madonna of the Shoe* to commemorate the miraculous transformation into gold of a shoe dedicated to it by a poor man. The altar is flanked by two *funerary lions* in red marble carved in the 13th century by an artist of the school of Benedetto Antelami, while the mosaics in the chapel are largely *rifacimenti* of the late 13th-century originals. Returning to the nave one can admire, on the inner wall, five splendid mosaic panels of *Ezekiel, Solomon*, a *Madonna at Prayer, David* and *Isaiah*, executed in the early 13th century by an artist who harmonised elements from Byzantine and Romanesque sources. Among the 13th-century mosaics in the gallery above the nave are *Christ in the Garden of Gethsemane* in six episodes, outstanding examples of Venetian early 13th century mosaic art.

Further on there are other fragments of the old paving depicting animals and, on the pillar to the right, a bas-relief of the *Madonna and Child*, probably 12th-century work, called the *Madonna del Bacio* because at one time it was a custom among believers to kiss it. Continuing along the right arm of the **southern transept**, which preserves, on upper gallery, fine late 13th-century mosaics. They depict two episodes on "civic" themes: *Prayer for the Discovery of St. Mark's Body* and *Discovery of St. Mark's Body*, and are also interesting as illustrating the basilica as it was in the period. At the end of the nave opens the *Door of the Treasury*, below a Moorish arch containing a 14th-century *Ecce Homo*. Passing beyond a door into the Doge's Palace—above it a great Gothic rose window with a radial pattern—we enter the **Chapel of the Sacrament**. This occupies the south aisle of the transept. It is fur-

One of the five mosaics on the wall of the right aisle of the middle arm, this depcts a Virgin Praying.

nished with a marble Baroque altar by Tommaso Contino (1617), and preserves traces of the original paving. On the left-hand pillar opposite the altar, note an *Angel* in relief: an eternal lamp once burned before it to commemorate the spot where, on 25 June 1094, St. Mark's body was found after being lost during the second reconstruction of the basilica. One then passes into the **Cappella di San Clemente**, which flanks the right side of the presbytery. Featuring a square ante-chapel and an apse, it is preceded by an *iconostasis* of red Verona marble composed of four columns linked by an architrave on which stand the statues of the *Madonna and Child* and *Four*

Saints by Jacobello and Pier Paolo Dalle Masegne (1397). Note, on the right-hand wall of the first chamber, a 12th-century mosaic with *Cain and Abel* above a fragment of a graffitto which seems to record the year (1159) when the marble decoration of the basilica was completed. In the pillar on the left is set the *Tabernacle of the Relics*, its marble structure enriched with statuettes from the circle of the Dalle Masegne family. The mosaic of *St. Clement* on the vault of the apisdal recess is in 12th century Byzantine style, while the two marble panels of the *altar* date from 1465 and 1538: they represent respectively a *Madonna with St. Mark and St. Bernardino* and *St. An-*

Mosaic in the Zen chapel depicting the Burial of St. Mark in Alexandria.

drew, *St. Jacob and St. Nicholas Venerated by Doge Andrea Gritti*.

This chapel leads into the **presbytery**, bounded towards the nave by a monumental marble *iconostasis*. It consists of a polychrome marble parapet richly worked and eight gilded columns linked by an architrave. On this stand a row of *statues* and a majestic *cross* by the Venetian goldsmith Marco Benato, in bronze and silver and enriched with figures in relief that represent *Christ with the Symbols of the Evangelists* on one side and *St. Mark with the Doctors of the Church* on the other. The marble statues of the *Madonna, St. George*, and the *Apostles* flanking it were carved by Iacobello and Pier Paolo Dalle Masegne in 1394.

At the sides of the iconostasis, resting on the side pillars of the presbytery, are two early 14th-century ambos, made largely by reusing materials from various ages and places. The one on the right, called the *Ambo of the Relics*, is polygonal in structure and supported by seven marble columns and a parapet of slabs of prophyry and diaspore, including, near the staircase, a fine Byzantine *pluteus* (10th century) decorated with peacocks. The left-hand *ambo* consists of two superimposed pulpits, the lower for the Epistle and the upper for the Gospel. Note also the fine 12th century Byzantine sculptures of an *angel* and an *eagle* supporting their respective reading stand.

The presbytery is polarised by the great altar on which stands an urn containing the remains of St. Mark. Above it is a *ciborium*, composed

---

Mosaic in the Cappella di San Clemente. The Priest Teodoro and the Monk Stauracio consign St. Mark's body to the merchants Rustico di Torcello and Buono di Malamocco.

The **technique of enamelling** involves two different phases, the making of polychrome glass pastes and their application to a metal surface. In the first phase materials like silica, potassium soda, red lead and colouring

materials are fused together and then cooled and reduced to powder. In the second phase the paste is moistened and poured onto a metal surface in moulds. If the pattern is then incised the technique is called "champlevé"; if the

enamel is enclosed in strips of wood or metal the technique is called "cloisonné," and this is the method used for the *Pala d'Oro* in the Basilica of San Marco.

of a cross-vaulted canopy supported by four alabaster columns completely covered with reliefs, perhaps from the mid-13th century, representing *Gospel Stories*. Behind it is the celebrated *Pala d'Oro* (the retable of the high altar), by Gian Paolo Boninsegna in 1342. He created a twofold structure of gold with architectural compartments within which he set plaquettes of enamels, precious stones, pearls (255 sapphires, 183 amethysts, 75 rubies, 175 agates, 34 topazes, 16 cornelians, 13 diaspores,) some of them used for earlier altarpieces for the church dating from 976–978, 1105 and 1209. In the middle of the upper range there is a great 11th–12th century Byzantine enamel of the *Archangel Michael* surrounded by sixteen medals of *Saints* from previous periods. A set of arches contain a beautiful series of Byzantine enamels of the 11th–12th centuries depicting (left) *Christ's Entry into Jerusalem*, the *Descent into Limbo*, and the *Crucifixion*; while on the right are the *Ascension*, the *Pentecoste*, and the *Death of the Virgin*.

The lower range is divided into three panels surrounded on three sides by small plaquettes depicting *Gospel Stories* and *Stories of St. Mark*; the enamels at the centre represent *Christ Blessing* (12th century) surrounded by *Evangelists and Angels*; they flank the *Preparation of the Throne*. These side panels, set within small niches, represent figures of *Angels*, *Prophets* and *Apostles*. Note, finally, in the centre, below, the *Virgin*, the *Empress Irene* and the *Doge Ordelafo Falier* (originally the figure represented the Emperor John Comnenus II).

At the centre of the apse at the rear is the *Altar of the Sacrament*: the tabernacle door is by Jacopo Sansovino, who also executed the *Sacristy Door* that opens on the left, with bronze panels of the *Resurrection of Christ* and the *Deposition*, surrounded by a frame decorated with figures of *Evangelists* and *Prophets* and

portraits (*Titian;Veronese; Sansovino*). Also by Sansovino are the bronze statuettes of the *Evangelists* on the balustrade beside the ciborium, together with figures of *Patriarchs* by Girolamo Plaiari (c. 1614).

Of the greatest artistic and historical interest are the wall mosaics between the windows of the apse, with *St. Nicholas, St. Peter, St. Mark* and *St. Ermagora*. They are the oldest mosaics in St. Mark's and may well be earlier than the fire of 1106 that destroyed many of the mosaics in the basilica.

One of the four columns of Oriental alabaster carved with biblical scenes which support the ciborium on the High Altar.

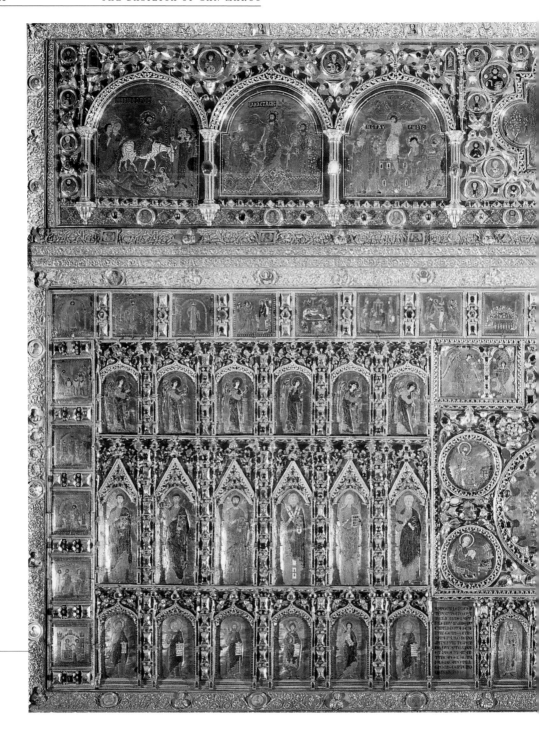

The Pala d'Oro,
Gothic goldsmith's
work enclosing enamels
from earlier periods.

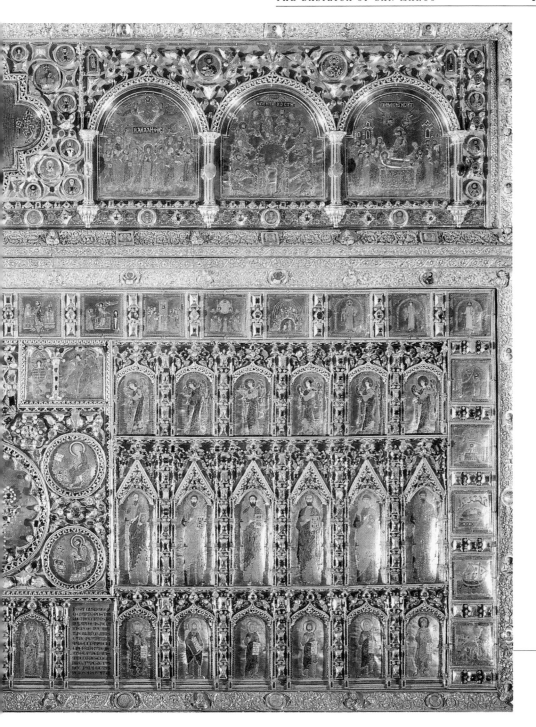

Finally, in the right-hand gallery note the fine early 13th-century mosaic of the *Removal of the Body of St. Mark from Alexandria*.

Leaving the presbytery one enters the **Cappella di San Pietro**, the counterpart in furnishings and plan to that of San Clemente. It, too, is preceded by a marble *iconostasis* complete with statues of the *Madonna* and four *Saints*, in this case by members of the Dalle Masegne family and others. On a pillar at its right side it preserves a marble *Tabernacle of the Saint's Relics* in Decorated Gothic style adorned with statuettes. The bas-relief on the altar dates from the 14th century: it represents *St. Peter Reverenced by Two Procurators*. The mosaic in the vault over the apse, which represents *St. Peter*, is from the 13th century. From here one passes into the **sacristy**, erected by Giorgio Spavento in 1486–1490 and decorated with Cinquecento mosaics, some after cartoons by Titian. Also of interest is the late-15th century carved and inlaid furniture.

Leaving the chapel by a staircase that opens on the left of the ambo, one can descend to the 11th-century **crypt,** which underlies the presbytery and flanking rooms. A triple apse surmounted by cross-vaults carried on marble columns is furnished with an *altar* near which, during restoration work in 1811, was discovered the urn with the bones of St. Mark.

Returning upstairs, we enter the **left transept** with, set against the right-hand pillar, the admirable Quattrocento altar of St. Paul with a fine marble altarpiece of the *Conversion of St. Paul*. The right aisle holds the **Cappella della Madonna Nicopeia** ("bringer of victory"): on the altar is a panel of a *Madonna and Child* by a Byzantine-Comnenian artist active during the early 12th century. Tradition has it that this painting, like others of the same kind taken into war by the Byzantine emperors, reached Venice in 1204 with other loot from the fourth Crusade. At the end is the **Cappella di**

Sant' Isidoro, built by order of Doge Andrea Dandolo in 1354 to hold the remains of St. Isidore, brought from Chios more than two centuries earlier. It is decorated with 14th-century mosaics illustrating the *Stories of St. Isidore*, and there are interesting marble reliefs on the arcosolium of the end wall.

Above the altar is the sarcophagus holding the *relics of St. Isidore*, decorated with carvings of scenes from his life.

Adjoining this is the **Cappella della Madonna dei Mascoli**, begun in 1430; it takes its name from the fact that it used to be the property of an all-male confraternity. The altar is in Decorated Gothic style, dated 1430 and surmounted by a triptych with statues of the *Virgin between St. Mark and St. John the Baptist*. The mosaics date from 1430–1450 and illustrate scenes from the *Life of the Virgin*, in a style that in some ways looks forward to the Re-

Pala d'Oro, *enamel*
of the Archangel Michael
(19 × 12 cm).

Pala d'Oro, *enamel*
of the translation
of the body of St. Mark
(13 × 13 cm).

The altar of the chapel of the "Mascoli" in Decorated Gothic style, attributed to Giovanni Bon.

naissance. They are mostly by Michele Giambono, except the *Visitation*, perhaps painted to a cartoon by Jacopo Bellini, and the *Death of the Virgin*, probably a collaboration between Giambono and Andrea del Castagno.

Further along the left aisle we come to the **Portale della Madonna** and, on the opposite side, a Romanesque holy-water stoup from the 12th century. Of particular interest is the nearby allegorical fragment of paving, depicting *Hens Carrying a Fox on a Stick*, apparently an allegory of *Craft Defeated by Vigilance*. Also of great interest are the early 12th-century mosaics covering the walls of the gallery above, with *Stories of the Virgin*, mostly from the Apocryphal Gospels.

Reaching the **left aisle** of the middle arm we find, on the right-hand wall, the so-called *Madonna dello Scoppio*, a 14th-century bas-relief of a *Virgin and Child*. Further on are five very fine mosaic panels containing the figures of *Christ, Jeremiah, Mica, Jole*, and *Hosea* who, like those in the opposite aisle, are admirable examples of early 13th century Italian mosaic.

A tour of the basilica can also take in the **Tesoro di San Marco** and **Museo di San Marco**. The Treasury contains the rich treasure of the basilica, a collection of sacred furnishings and liturgical and other items (including cups, chalices, amphorae, carpets and hangings), some of which were brought from Constantinople as part of the booty of the fourth Crusade (1204). Particularly of note a silver *perfume censer* in the form of a 12th- to 13th-century church, two 11th-century ikons depicting the *Archangel Michael*, and precious silver-gilt altarpieces, one from the late 13th century donated by Pope Gregory XII in 1408 to the Cathedral of San Pietro di Castello.

The Museum occupies a number of rooms above the south atrium. In the first room there are many mosaic fragments from the basilica, illuminated Cinquecento choir-books, 14th century Flemish hangings and a contrabass made by the Luthier Gaspare da Salò.

The second room has more mosaics and the *Pala feriale*, an altarpiece which was used to cover the *Pala d'Oro* on week-days: it is the work of Paolo Veneziano and his sons Luca and Giovanni, bears the date 1345 and represents (above) *Christ and the Virgin with Saints* and (below) *Stories of St. Mark*. In the third room there are more altarpieces and important 15th

Jacopo Sansovino, door of the sacristy with panels depicting the Deposition *and* Resurrection of Christ.

century Persian carpets woven of silk, gold and silver, gifts from the Persian ambassadors in 1603 and 1622. Particularly precious is the fragment of a Flemish hanging from the 15th century depicting the *Coronation of a Holy Roman Emperor*, a gift to the basilica by Cardinal Zen.

Paolo Veneziano with his sons Luca and Giovanni, Pala Feriale. *Museo di San Marco.*

Christ Appears to St. Mark in Prison. Detail of the Pala Feriale.

The Museum also contains a sculptural group (still partly gilded) of the *Quadriga* formerly on the balcony of the facade of San Marco, attributed by some scholars to Roman artists of the 4th–3rd centuries BC and by others to the period of Constantine (3rd–4th centuries AD). The four horses, the sole quadriga which has survived from ancient times, were looted by the Venetians from the Hippodrome of Constantinople during the Fourth Crusade and brought to Venice in 1204.

In 1798 Napoleon carried them off to Paris, where they remained until 1815; they were first placed before the Tuileries and then on the triumphal arch of the Carousel.

This altarpiece was called the **Pala feriale** because it functioned as an altar-frontal to cover the *Pala d'Oro* during week days. It is signed and dated "M.C.C.C.XLV. MENSE APRILIS:DIE: XXII. MAGISTER. PAULUS. CUM. LUCA. E. IOHANNE. FILIIS SUIS. PINXERUNT. HOC. OPUS." It has two registers of seven squares each, representing in the upper register (from the left) *St. George*, *St. Mark*, the *Mater Dolorosa* and *St. John the Evangelist*, *St. Peter* and *St. Nicholas* who face *Christ*, while on the bottom register are the *Stories of St. Mark*. Scholars write about the difference in style between the upper register, which is still linked to the Byzantine tradition and the lower one, where there is a lively narrative and chronistic atmosphere.

The Doge's Palace

The earliest permanent settlements in the lagoon of Venice seem to date back to the period following the fall of the Western Roman Empire (476), caused by the inroads of barbarian peoples. These early settlements were gradually consolidated until they were seen as outposts of the Byzantine Empire.

In the 7th century, the first Dux or, in Venetian dialect, Doge was installed, probably with the approval of the Eastern Emperor, who made the local administration autonomous. This role, suspended at various times due to rivalry between various families, became permanent in the mid-8th century on the election of Doge Teodato Ipato.

By the start of the 9th century, Venice was increasingly independent, isolated by its distance from the capital and confirmed by a religious difference: the dedication of the city to St. Theodore, the patron saint of Byzantium, was replaced by the cult of the Apostle Mark, whose remains, according to later historians, were supposedly preserved in the city.

In 810 Doge Angelo Partecipazio moved the seat of government from Malamocco to Rivoalto, and sought a suitable location for the organs of government of the new state. A site on land belonging to him on the islands of Rivoalto was chosen and at building commenced on the *palatium ducis*. This is still the site of the Doge's Palace, though nothing remains of the 9th-century structure. We know nothing about the form of the original palace; but we do know that in the 13th century it had a main block that was purely defensive in purpose, laid out on a square ground plan, a sort of mediaeval castle. Of the older structure, some parts of the four corner towers remain.

In the 10th century the palace was partially destroyed by fire during a revolt against the Doge Pietro Candiano IV. Its reconstruction, under Doge Sebastiano Ziani (1172-1178), eschewed defence in favour of a typically Venetian-Byzantine style. The palace was thus adapted to the contemporary changes in the city's institutions and the creation of new officers of state, who shared power with the Doge. Hence the need for greater space and more chambers than before. An 18th-century print shows us how the Doge's Palace was originally structured.

Along the side on Piazzetta San Marco there was the building known as *ad jus reddendum* (the Law Courts), with a colonnade on the ground floor and a loggia opening on the first storey; the offices were on the upper floor. The side facing the quay had the *palatium commune* for deliberative assemblies: this was made by

Statue of Eve on one of the corners of the Doge's Palace.

Doge's Palace, facade on the quay.

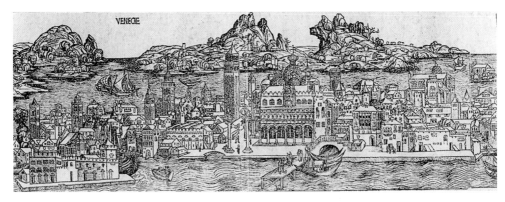

adapting the outer wall of the old building to serve as an inner wall, and then building on one side out towards the Piazzetta and on the other towards the tower on the corner of the Ponte della Paglia. Few traces remain of this phase of construction: all one can see is a base in Istrian stone and some brick paving laid in a herringbone pattern.

Further extensions became necessary in the late 13th century. In 1297 the *Serrata* of the Maggior Consiglio considerably increased membership of the legislative assembly from 400 to 1,200. Because of the need to enlarge the council chamber, it was decided to take in the adjoining rooms rather than build a new one on the upper storey. Work began in about 1340 under Doge Bartolomeo Gradenigo (1339–1343) and was completed in 1362, despite delays caused by the plague of 1348. For this phase of the work we have the names of some of the craftsmen: in 1361, for instance, documents mention a certain Filippo Calendario, stonemason, and Pietro Basejo, *magister prothus*, who must have been assisted by numerous other masons and sculptors, given the rapidity with which work progressed.

The extensions also affected other parts of the building and when they were finally complete the palace must have looked much as we see it today.

In 1424, under Doge Francesco Foscari (1423–1457), it was decided to rebuild what remained of the palace of Doge Ziani facing onto Piazzetta San Marco, both to improve its stability and for aesthetic reasons. The new building was designed as a continuation of the Doge's Palace. It starts from the relief of *Justice*, level with the thirteenth column of the loggia, and unites the end of the Sala del Maggior Consiglio with the main entrance to the palace, flanked by the two original structures. This new building—none of the names of the workmen are recorded—has a colonnade on the ground level and loggia above, both in the outer elevation and the elevation on the courtyard.

On the same floor as the Sala del Maggior Consiglio there is a huge chamber, known as the Sala della Libreria (later the Sala dello Scrutinio). The windows and pinnacles of the gable repeat the decorative motifs on the sea facade. The elevation facing Piazzetta San Marco was completed with the construction of the Porta della Carta (1438–1442) by Giovanni and Bartolomeo Bon.

It was later decided to rebuild the part of the palace to which access was provided by this new door. The construction of the lobby, known as the *androne Foscari*, took some years, as is shown by the presence of the arms of Doge

Anonymous, Perspective plan of the city of Venice, 15th century.

Cristoforo Moro (1462–1471); work was completed under Doge Giovanni Mocenigo (1478–1485).

In 1483 a serious fire damaged much of the palace and once more extensive reconstruction was necessary. A building arose on the same site, joining the Ponte di Canonica with the Ponte di Paglia: this work was entrusted to Antonio Rizzo, who also designed and constructed the staircase opposite the Arco Foscari.

By 1497 work had progressed as far as the second arch after the staircase, and was completed as far as the Doge's apartments in 1501 when Agostino Barbarigo died, after taking possession of the new building. Meanwhile Antonio Rizzo had fled from Venice after being accused of embezzlement. The work was then turned over to "maestro Pietro Lombardo," who was commissioned to oversee the completion of the sculptural decoration of the facade and the Scala dei Giganti.

In the following years setbacks to the Venetian state slowed work, so that when Antonio Abbondi lo Scarpagnino took over from Pietro Lombardo, little progress had been made. In 1531 it was finally decided to rebuild the old part of the palace; and ten years later a passage was built to link the Doge's apartment with the Sala del Maggior Consiglio. The arms of Doge Francesco Donà, elected in 1545, mark the completion of the marble façade on the ground and upper storeys. In the years that followed, the old wooden staircase that linked the buildings on the canal was replaced and work was only completed in 1559, under the supervision of Pietro Piccolo.

Finally the palace was complete, and each administrative organ had its own chambers. The installation on the staircase of the two great statues of *Mars* and *Neptune* by Sansovino in 1565 can be said to have marked the end of this important phase of work.

Courtyard of the Doge's Palace, 18th-century print.

In 1574 another fire destroyed part of the chambers on the second floor. Particularly badly damaged were the Sala delle Quattro Porte, the ante-chamber to the Collegio, the Collegio itself and the Senate, but fortunately without harming the main structure. The panelling, and above all the decorations, were immediately repaired. But as soon as work was complete in 1577 another devastating fire damaged the Sala dello Scrutinio and Sala del Maggior Consiglio, completely destroying the paintings by Bellini, Pordenone and Titian that had decorated them.

There were various plans for refurbishing the wing; finally it was decided to accept a proposal by Giovanni Antonio Rusconi, who set to work to restore its original appearance. The work was rapidly completed between 1579 and 1580, under Doge Nicolò da Ponte. Until then the palace had contained not only the Doge's residence, government chambers and law courts, but also housed the prisons (on the ground floor to right and left of the Porta del Frumento).

It was only in the late-16th century that Antonio da Ponte ordered the construction of the Prigioni Nuove, designed by Antonio Contin. They were completed by around 1600 and linked by the Bridge of Sighs. The transfer of the prisons to the new buildings vacated space on the ground floor of the palace. Restructuring by Monopola at the start of the 17th century completely altered the ground floor with the creation of a colonnade like that on the Renaissance facade. At this time the Scala Foscari was also pulled down and replaced by the present internal staircase; and in the empty space between the facade of the Arco Foscari in the courtyard and the corner of the palace, Monopola built a facade with an arcade on the ground and upper storeys, terminating in the structure containing the clock (1615).

The functions of the Doge's Palace changed at the end of the 18th century, when the Austrian domination replaced the French. In 1807 it became the Court of Appeal; in 1812 the Marcian Library was moved to the Sala del Maggior Consiglio and later to the Doge's Apartments. The library was soon joined by the Archaeological Museum.

In the 1860s restoration work done, but it was only in 1908 that the library was moved to its

present premises, and in 1918 the Archaeological Museum was also transferred. In 1924 the Italian state, owner of the palace, turned the building over to the municipality, and it was opened to the public as a museum.

The oldest part of the Doge's Palace is now the **facade** facing the quay, with its 13th-century sculptures at the corners of the building. They are attributed to Filippo Calendario or certain Lombard artists, like the Raverti or Bregno families. On the side facing the Ponte della Paglia they represent *Tobias and the Angel Raphael* (above) and the *Drunkenness of Noah*; towards Piazzetta San Marco are the *Archangel Michael* (above) and *Adam and Eve*. Both on this side of the palace and the side facing the Piazzetta there used to be a number of 14th-century capitals, replaced by copies in the 19th century and now in the Museo dell'Opera. The central balcony dates from the 15th century: it was dated (1400–1404) by Pier Paolo Dalle Masegne

Doge's Palace, facade facing the Piazzetta.

"Filippo Calendario," Aristotele Dialecticus *on the capital of the Sapienti.*

*View of the Doge's
Palace.*

*Detail of the statue
of Eve at a corner
of the Doge's Palace.*

*Doge's Palace seen from
the Ponte della Paglia.*

*Doge's Palace, the
openwork of the loggia.*

and harmonises well with the 14th-century architecture of the facade. The coping of the balcony was refashioned in 1579, when the statue of *Justice* by Alessandro Vittoria was added to replace the original, by an earthquake in 1511. The statue of *St. George* is an 18th-century work by Giovanni Battista Pellegrini. The other statues represent *St. Theodore*, the *Cardinal Virtues*, *St. Mark*, *St. Peter* and *St. Paul*. On the facade facing Piazzetta San Marco, near the thirteenth column, a bas-relief of *Justice Enthroned* has been inserted among the pierced *tondi* of the loggia. The balcony at the centre of the side on the Piazzetta was built in the early 16th century in imitation of the balcony facing the quay. The sculptural treatment of the corner towards the Porta della Carta is extremely effective, representing the *Judgment of Solomon* and, above, the *Archangel Gabriel*: critics now attribute these works to Bartolomeo Bon. It is likely that the overall scheme embodied in the various groups of sculpture is meant to express the principal features of Venetian society, while suggesting parallels between the Doge's Palace and the Palace of Solomon and also representing it as the seat of Justice.

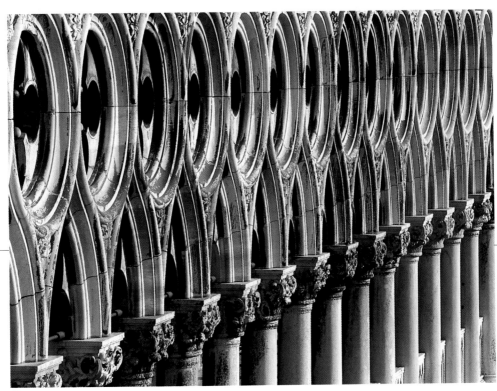

Work began on the **Porta della Carta**, the monumental entrance to the palace, in 1438 and continued for the next four years. On the architrave is carved OPUS BARTHOLOMEI. The name of this entrance seems to be due to the fact that public scribes would gather here, or perhaps public records ("cartarum") were stored nearby.

In Decorated Gothic style, it is remarkable for its rich sculptures and ornate surfaces, which were originally painted or gilded. It is flanked by two pinnacles within which are two figures of *Cardinal Virtues*, attributed to Bregno, and above is the bust of *St. Mark the Evangelist*, surmounted by the figure of *Justice* bearing its iconographic attributes of a sword and scales.

Above the cornice over the door is Francesco Foscari—under whose dogeship the work was carried out—kneeling before the lion of St. Mark. This is a work by Luigi Ferrari and was commissioned to replace the original destroyed in 1797.

Admission to the Doge's Palace today is by the Porta del Frumento, on the side facing the quay.

The Porta della Carta.

The Porta della Carta, detail with Doge Francesco Foscari kneeling in front of the lion of St. Mark.

Following page, above *Filippo Calendario, capital.*

Following page, below *View of the room in the Museo dell'Opera of the Doge's Palace.*

The **Museo dell'Opera** contains thirteen capitals from the palace's outer loggia: they were replaced with copies during restoration work in 1876–1887. Twelve of them, with anthropomorphic decorations and some with Latin inscriptions, date from the phase of work that began in 1340 and scholars now generally attribute them to Filippo Calendario; one is early 15th-century work.

Among the capitals from the loggia there is a very fine one with the *Creation of Adam and Eve, The Planets and their Houses*. The rooms in the museum also have twenty-nine capitals from the loggia, all dating from c. 1340–1450, notable for their highly decorative qualities and lack of inscriptions.

The two facades of the east wing of the palace, which look onto the courtyard and canal, were both built at about the same time, and can be dated with some precision by the arms of the doges reigning during the various phases of work.

The facade onto the canal goes back to the dogeship of Giovanni Mocenigo (1478–1485), whose arms appear on the pilaster at the entrance to the Doge's chamber. The facade looking onto the courtyard is slightly later, as shown by the arms of Doge Marco Bar-

barigo (1485–1486) on the first capital on the corner of the Cortile dei Senatori. Under his successor, Agostino Barbarigo (1486–1501) work proceeded steadily on both facades and reached the seventh arch of the arcade after the Scala dei Giganti, up to the piano nobile.

Meanwhile work continued on the interior, and must have been well-advanced by 1498, the year when Rizzo fled. In 1514 it had already reached the eleventh arch, while the arms of

Francesco Donà (1545–1553) placed a little further on seem to suggest that work had slowed down on the courtyard front, while the arms of Leonardo Loredan (1501–1521) on the canal facade indicate that work had made more progress on that side. In the courtyard there are also the *well-heads* bearing the signatures of the craftsmen who cast them, Nicolò de Conti and Albergeto.

On the south side, running the whole length of the courtyard, is the Renaissance facade built after the fire of 1483 and completed in the mid-16th century. Access to the upper storeys of the Doge's Palace is by the **Scala dei Censori**, on which work began in 1525 to replace the previous unroofed outdoor staircase; it leads from the ground floor to the second *piano nobile*; it was probably designed by Scarpagnino.

On the upper storey is the loggia, which is distinguished by the *Bocche di Leone* inserted in the walls and the plaque of Alessandro Vittoria, commemorating the visit of King Henri III of France.

The **Bocche di Leone** on the walls of various parts of the Doge's Palace, in particular the loggia, Sala della Bussola and Sala della Quarantia Criminal, served for delivering anonymous accusations. They had the form of a lion's head—hence their name—and the open mouth was the slit for letters. Each Magistracy had its own Bocche di Leone.

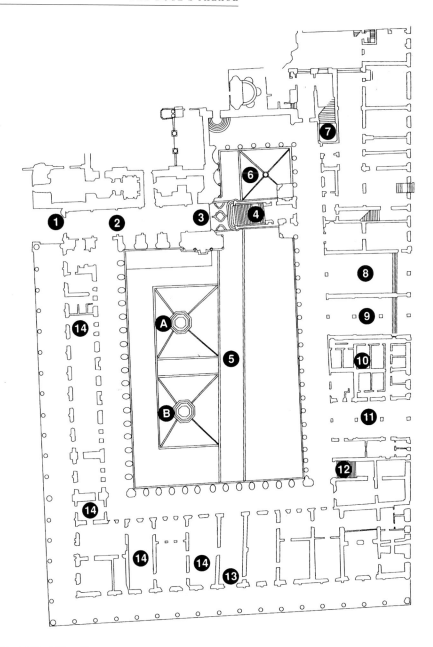

Preceding page
*Courtyard of the Doge's
Palace facing the
Basilica of San Marco.*

Ground-floor plan
1. Porta della Carta
2. Porticato Foscari
3. Arco Foscari
4. Scala dei Giganti
5. Courtyard
6. Cortile dei Senatori
7. Scala dei Senatori
8–9. Riva Barbarigo
10. Well-heads

11. Riva Donà
12. Scala dei Censori
13. Porta del Frumento
14. Museo dell'Opera
A. Alberghetti's well
B. Nicolò dei Conti's well

Scala d'Oro
and the Doge's Apartment

The gap between the Doge's residence and the Palazzo di Giustizia was filled by constructing the **Scala d'Oro**, designed by Jacopo Sansovino in 1538, after the most famous architects of the day—Palladio, Sammicheli, Rusconi—had been approached with the commission. It was completed in 1559 by Scarpagnino under Doge Lorenzo Priuli, whose arms appear on the inner side of the archway. The arms on the outer side are of Doge Andrea Gritti, under whom work began. The structure consists of various flights of steps leading to the Doge's Apartments on the first floor on the canal side, and then to the second floor, where there are the great assembly chambers and those used for the high offices of the Venetian state. At the sides of the doorway are two statues, *Hercules Killing the Hydra* and *Atlantis*, by Tiziano Aspetti. Ascending the **Scala d'Oro**, on the first floor we come to the **Doge's Apartment** (see the plan on page 82), completely rebuilt after the fire of 1483 to designs by Antonio Rizzo and Pietro Solari, called Lombardo, under the Doges Giovanni Mocenigo and Marco and Agostino Barbarigo, on whose death some details were still incomplete. However, the suite must have been in use by 1492.

The chambers are largely devoid of furniture because furnishings were regarded as the doge's private property and hence on election each doge brought his own and his heirs removed them at his death. At the centre of the

suite is a large central chamber running the whole length of the palace and set at right angles to another long chamber with three smaller rooms on either side.

The Scala d'Oro.

Sala degli Scarlatti

The first chamber as one enters from the Scala d'Oro is the **Sala degli Scarlatti**, once used as an ante-chamber for the doge's councillors. Of the ancient interior there still remains the carved ceiling, designed and probably executed by Biagio and Pietro da Faenza. Between the two windows is the chimney-piece, the work of Antonio and Tullio Lombardo, dating from c. 1507: its classical decoration is typical of the taste of the period.

The two marble reliefs above the doors depicit *Doge Loredan Before the Virgin* and the *Virgin and Child*. The various rooms of the Doge's Apartment are hung with paintings, some of which come from other rooms in the palace, while others are of unknown provenance.
In the Sala degli Scarlatti are works like Giuseppe Salviati's *Resurrection* and Titian's *Madonna with Child and Angels*, whose dimensions suggest it must originally have adorned the landing of the staircase that leads from the Cortile dei Senatori to the first-floor loggia.

Sala delle Mappe, Sala Grimani and Sala Erizzo

The **Sala delle Mappe** (or **Sala dello Scudo**) is decorated with a series of maps painted on canvas in the Cinquecento, but restored in the 18th century. The **Sala Grimani**, named after Doge Marino Grimani (1595–1606), whose arms are at the centre of the ceiling, is decorated with a frieze painted with a series of allegorical figures, including *Venice* and *St. Mark*. The splendid carved ceiling ane fireplace are original, by Lombardo, while the stucco embrasure was added under the Doge Pasquale Cicogna (1585–1595), whose arms it bears. On the walls are three paintings of the *Lion* of St. Mark, one by Jacobello del Fiore (signed and dated 1415), one by Donato Veneziano (1459) and one by Vittore Carpaccio (signed and dated 1516). The next room is the **Sala Erizzo**, decorated with a frieze with *putti* and symbols of war. On the walls are paintings, including the *Presentation at the Temple*, *Noah's Arc* and the *Ascent to Calvary* attributed by the critics to Gerolamo Bassano.

From the Sala degli Stucchi to the Sala degli Scudieri

The **Sala degli Stucchi** (or **Priuli**) was originally laid out for Doge Lorenzo Priuli (1556–1559) and subsequently refurbished in the 18th century by Doge Lorenzo Grimani (1741–1752), who added, among other things, the stucco decorations of walls and ceiling. It is adorned by various paintings, including a *Portrait of Henri III* attributed to Tintoretto, a *Holy Family*, an *Ascent to Calvary*, a *Noli Me Tangere*, a *Circumcision* and *Christ Praying in the Garden of Gethsemene* by Giuseppe Salviati, and an *Adoration of the Shepherds* by L. Bassano.

The **Sala dei Filosofi**, which serves as a passageway, has an 18th century stucco ceiling and is decorated with twelve canvases with portraits of philosophers painted in the 18th century and originally intended for the Biblioteca Marciana.

From this room a small staircase joins the Doge's Apartments with the chapel above. Over the staircase door is a *St. Christopher* by Titian (c. 1523). The **chapel**, at present closed to the public, was designed by Scamozzi in 1593. On the altar is a statue of the *Madonna and Child* by Jacopo Sansovino. The walls are decorated with *trompe l'œil* architecture and the ceiling with allegorical ornaments.

On the walls of the **Sala Corner** there are paintings related to the history of the Corner family. The next room contains the *Dead Christ* by Giovanni Bellini. The **Sala degli Scudieri**, originally an antechamber, has been stripped of its original decoration and now contains two paintings by Domenico Tintoretto.

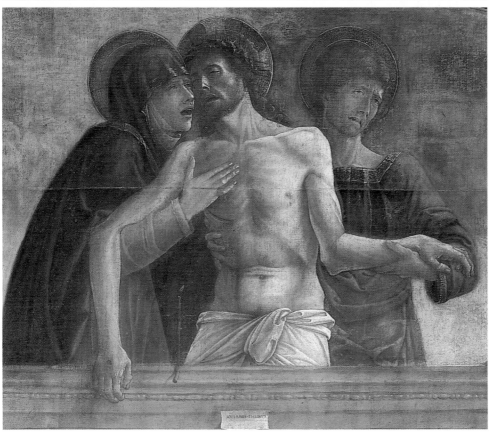

Giovanni Bellini,
Dead Christ, *full view*
and detail, signed
JOHANES BELLINUS.

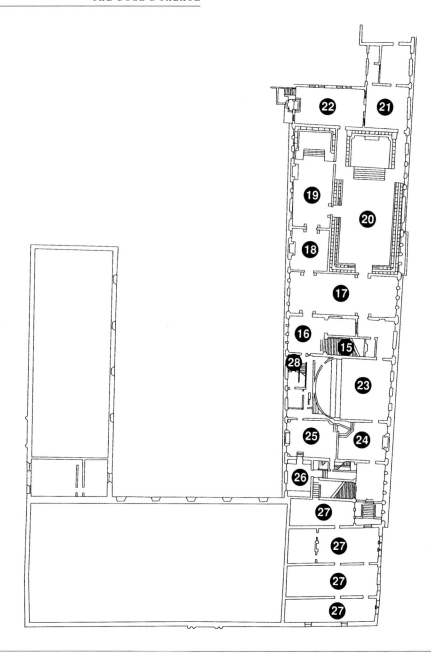

Atrio Quadrato

Continuing up the Scala d'Oro to the second floor, we reach the **Atrio Quadrato**. This is a fairly small chamber that serves as a hallway to the great state-rooms. The decorative scheme was completed in the mid-16th century under Doge Gerolamo Priuli (1559–1567), whose portrait on the ceiling was painted by Jacopo Tintoretto (1564–1565). The portrait is flanked by biblical scenes and *putti*, by artists of the school of Tintoretto. During the dogeship of Priuli, the walls were adorned with four canvases by Tintoretto, now in the Sala del Anticollegio. In their place are other 16th-century works: *St. John Writing the Book of Revelations* and the *Annunciation to the Shepherds*, ascribed by scholars to Paolo Veronese and Gerolamo Bassano; the *Expulsion of Adam and Eve from Eden*, attributed doubtfully to Paolo Veronese or Paolo Fiammingo, and *Christ Praying in the Garden of Gethsemane* of the school of Veronese.

Paolo Veronese (attributed to), St. John Writing the Book of Revelations. *Atrio Quadrato.*

Sala delle Quattro Porte

The next room is the **Sala delle Quattro Porte**, clearly having the function of an anteroom, giving access to other chambers. It runs the whole depth of the palace and was formerly the venue for meetings of the College, and hence of the *fanti* (or ushers). Its present arrangement, with the four doors which give it its name, columns standing out from the walls, the statues above and the mullioned windows opening onto both Rio di Canonica and the inner courtyard, is the result of its restructuring in 1483. The décor was altered at various times and finally completely renewed after the fire of 1574. The commission for the new design was given to Andrea Palladio and Giovanni Rusconi, and the work was executed by Antonio da Ponte. The barrel-vaulted ceiling is decorated with white stucco and gilding, in harmony with the refined taste of the age, and is ascribed to Bombarda (1575–1577). The frescoes on the ceiling are by Tintoretto, painted between 1578 and 1581 and based on a scheme devised by Francesco Sansovino. The frescoes in the circular panels in the ceiling represent *Juno Offering Venice the Peacock and Thunderbolt* and

Venice Breaking the Chains of Captivity; the one in the centre represents *Venice Symbolically Receiving Dominion Over the Adriatic from Jove*; while the eight ovals depict the cities and regions of the mainland (*Verona, Istria, Brescia, Padua, Friuli, Treviso, Vicenza, Altino*). The ovals of the lunettes represent *Philosophers*. The four portals, designed by Palladio, are surmounted by groups of sculpture alluding to the chamber into which they lead. The wall decoration, perhaps

begun by Titian in the mid-16th century, was completed later (1595–1600) under Doge Marco Grimani. The canvases represent *Doge Antonio Grimani Kneeling before Religion* and *St. Mark* (begun by Titian and completed by his nephew Marco Vecellio); the *Venetians under Gattamelata Defeat the Visconti and Retake Verona* (by Giovanni Contarini); the *Legates of Nuremberg Receive the Laws of Venice from Doge Loredan* (by Carlo and Gabriele Caliari); *Henri III Arrives at Venice, Welcomed by the Doge*

Sala delle Quattro Porte, view.

Andrea Vicentino, The Doge and the Patriarch Welcoming Henri III, King of France to Venice, detail. Sala delle Quattro Porte.

Giambattista Tiepolo, Neptune Offering Venice the Riches of the Sea. Sala delle Quattro Porte.

and Patriarch (by Andrea Vicentino); *Doge Pasquale Cicogna Gives Audience to the Persian Ambassadors* (by C. and G. Caliari); above the windows onto the courtyard, *Venice Rising Above the World* (by Nicolò Bambini). Over the windows looking onto the canal is a work by Giambattista Tiepolo, *Neptune Offering Venice the Riches of the Sea* (1740), which replaced a painting by Tintoretto of *Venice Wed by Neptune Who Makes Her Queen of the Seas* that was damaged.

Sala del Anticollegio

The **Sala del Anticollegio** formed an anteroom for ambassadors and delegations waiting to be received by the Venetian state. The original decorative scheme, destroyed in the fire of 1574, was similar to that of the previous chamber.

The room was restored first by Palladio and then Scamozzi. The central fresco, *Venice Conferring Rewards and Honours,* is by Paolo Veronese. On the wall with the windows there is a chimney-piece in Palladian style, with statues by Scamozzi while the upper relief by Tiziano Aspetti. The walls, decorated down to 1716 with precious hangings, were later adorned with paintings. On the walls on either side of the door are the four canvases by Tintoretto originally painted for the Sala delle Quattro Porte (*Mercury and the Graces; Minerva Driving Back Mars; Ariadne Found by Bacchus; Vulcan's Forge*): these works have been interpreted as an allegory of the wise government of the Venetian Republic or, with greater probability, the harmonious succession of the seasons, identified with the harmony of good government.

The latter explanation seems to be corroborated by the *putti* representing the seasons in the previous room, beside the original location of these paintings. On the wall opposite the window is the *Rape of Europa* by Paolo Veronese and the *Return of Jacob with his Family* by Jacopo da Ponte, known as Bassano.

Access to the following room is through a doorway with a marble group attributed to Alessandro Vittoria.

Sala del Collegio

The **Sala del Collegio** was intended for assemblies of the Magistratura, called the "Pien Collegio," made up of the Signoria (the Minor Consiglio), the three *Capi della Quarantia*, and the three *Zonte* (the Savi del Consiglio, Savi di Terraferma and Savi degli Ordini). In this chamber they received ambassadors, and it was therefore necessary for it to be particularly splendid. In the mid-16th century the decoration consisted essentially of a painting by Domenico Zorzi depicting a Map of the Venetian Dukedom, a large clock and paintings, which Sansovino describes as by Giovanni Bellini and Titian, without, unfortunately, specifying their subjects. Records also show that there was another painting of the *Doge Lorenzo before the Holy Spirit* by Parrasio Micheli. The room's structure, already fixed in its main features soon after 1483, was completed with the present decorations after the fire of 1574, when it was rapidly redecorated. Francesco Bello and Andrea Faentin made the wooden wainscoting and carved ceiling (1576), to designs by Palladio, who may have collaborated with Rusconi (1574–1575). The splendid

Sala del Collegio, view towards the throne.

Paolo Veronese, Venice Enthroned with Justice and Peace. *Sala del Collegio, ceiling.*

paintings on the ceiling were executed by Veronese in 1575, and we know that the work was complete on the death of Doge Venier (1578). The fact that the decoration was completed so swiftly certainly helped to confer on the chamber its distinctive unity of design. The wooden benches and dais are original and hence quite different from those in the other rooms, nearly always much later work. The dossals, however, are of a later date, replacing those destroyed in the fire of 1574. The very fine chimney-piece between the windows is by Gerolamo Campagna (1585–1595). The cycle of paintings on the ceiling is meant to extol the power and glory of Venice: the central compartments represent *Mars and Neptune, Faith the Strength of the Republic*, and *Venice Enthroned with Justice and Peace*, works that can be confidently ascribed to Veronese. At the sides are depicted the *Virtues*, each with its symbolic attribute. Above the dais is a painting that represents *Sebastiano Venier Worshipping the Redeemer, with Saints*, also by Veronese. The walls are decorated with works by Tintoretto and his workshop (1581–1584): of particular interest is *Doge Andrea Gritti Worshipping the Virgin*, in which the master's hand seems evident.

Paolo Veronese, Faith the Strength of the Republic. *Sala del Collegio, ceiling.*

Sala del Senato

The **Sala del Senato**
(or **Sala dei Pregadi**) was
used for meetings of the
senate, the most ancient
institution in the Venetian
state. We have, unfortunately,
little information about the
original decoration of the
chamber, destroyed in the fire
of 1574. Renovation of this
room began some years later
than in the case of the others,
and was entrusted to Antonio
da Ponte, under Doge Pasqual
Cicogna, whose arms are
carved among the decorations
in the ceiling, the work of
Cristoforo Sorte in the 1580s.
Soon after the ceiling was
finished, the paintings were
added and were completed in
1595. The central panel, set
within a carved and gilded
surround, is the *Triumph
of Venice*, painted by Jacopo
and Domenico Tintoretto.
Also noteworthy are the
canvas of the *Dead Christ
Supported by Angels*, by
Tintoretto and assistants,
on the walls above the dais,
and on the opposite wall, the
*Doges Lorenzo and Gerolamo
Priuli Praying to the Virgin*
by Palma il Giovane. On the
wall opposite the windows are
two large clocks, one of which
bears the signs of the zodiac.

*Jacopo Tintoretto and
helpers,* Dead Christ
Supported by Angels,
Adoration of Doges
Pietro Lando and
Marcantonio Trevisan
with Their Patron Saints.
Sala del Senato.

Tommaso Dolabella,
Doge Pasquale Cicogna
Adores the Eucharist,
ceiling. Sala del Senato.

The **Sala del Senato** was
also known as the "Sala
dei Pregadi" because its
members were invited
("pregati") in writing to
attend council meetings.
The term "senato"
appeared in documents
only at the end of the
14th century, when the

number of members was
fixed at sixty. The
Serrata (or "closure")
of the Maggio Consiglio
in 1297 severely pruned
its powers, but the
patricians, hostile to the
idea of creating another
political organ, restored
to the Senate its original

political powers. The number of members increased rapidly in the 16th century by taking in the Quarantia, the Consiglio dei Dieci and a *Zonta* composed of sixty members, so that by the middle of the 16th century there were about 300 Senators. The Senate meetings were also attended by the Doge and his councillors as well as magistrates; it mainly dealt with political issues and also decided on declarations of war and extraordinary appointments.

View of the Sala del Senato.

*Jacopo Palma
il Giovane,* Venice
Receiving Gifts from
the Subject Provinces
Presented by Doge
Francesco Venier.
Sala del Senato.

*Jacopo Palma
il Giovane,* Doge Pietro
Loredan Beseeching
the Virgin for the End
of the Famine and
Victory Over the Turks.
Sala del Senato.

Sala del Consiglio dei Dieci

The **Sala del Consiglio dei Dieci** was restructured in 1533–1550 by Scarpagnino, and work at once began on the paintings, executed by Ponchino, the youthful Veronese and Zelotti. They first decorated the ceilings (1553–1554) with a cycle of illustrations probably devised by Daniele Barbaro and consisting largely of allegorical representations of the various functions of the councillors who met in this chamber. The ceiling has twenty-five compartments; the central one contains a 19th-century copy of the original work by Veronese, now in the Louvre. Among the finest paintings in this room are: the *Aged Oriental and a Young Woman* and *Juno Offering the Ducal Crown to Venice*, by Paolo Veronese, while the wall opposite the windows is adorned with a canvas by Aliense of the *Adoration of the Magi*. The painting of *Pope Alexander III Blessing Doge Ziani* was begun by Francesco Bassano but completed by assistants. The furnishings are at least in part original, but the seats of the members of the Council have been destroyed.

Paolo Veronese, Juno Offering the Ducal Crown to Venice. *Sala del Consiglio dei Dieci, ceiling.*

The **Consiglio dei Dieci** was a magistracy created in 1310 to deal with the Tiepolo-Querini conspiracy. It retained its emergency character for a long time, until in 1455 a decree of the Maggior Consiglio made it permanent. The Consiglio dei Dieci was empowered to investigate anyone who might threaten the security of the state. Its meetings were shrouded in mystery.
As its name implies, it consisted of ten ordinary members, appointed by the Senate and elected by the Maggior Consiglio, apart from the Doge himself.
After the fall of the Republic, the Sala dei Dieci was turned into a baqueting hall, and then under Austrian rule into a court of law.

Antonio Vassillachi, called l'Aliense, Adoration of the Magi. *Sala del Consiglio dei Dieci.*

Sala del Consiglio dei Dieci, view.

Paolo Veronese,
Aged Oriental and
Young Woman.
*Sala del Consiglio
dei Dieci, ceiling.*

Sala della Bussola

The **Sala della Bussola**
served as a vestibule and
waiting-room for the previous
chamber; it was refurbished
and decorated in the mid-16th
century. Note the chimney-
piece, decorated by Jacopo
Sansovino and pupils. The
paintings, some attributed
to Paolo Veronese, represent
scenes from Venetian history.
In the **Armoury** are displayed
numerous suits of armour
for warfare or jousting, as
well as swords, halbards, and
cross-bows (almost two
thousand weapons all told).
Of special interest is the
Bust of Doge Morosini by
Filippo Parodi in the Sala
Morosini.

*Armour of Henri IV
of France. Armoury.*

Sala della Bussola.

*Armoury,
Sala Morosini.*

The **Sala della Bussola**
takes its name from a
wooden compass. Its
purpose was to mask the
passage on the left
leading to the secret
chamber where meetings
were held between the
Tre Capi and the
Inquisitors.

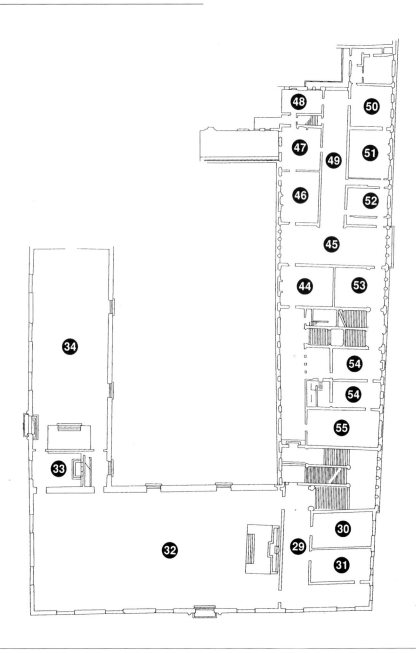

*Plan of the first floor
with the Doge's
Apartment*

29. Liagò
30. Sala della Quarantia
    Civil Vecchia
31. Sala dell'Armamento
    or del Guariento
32. Sale del Maggiore
    Consiglio
33. Sala della Quarantia
    Civil Nuova
34. Sala dello Scrutinia

Doge's Apartment
44. Sala degli Scarlatti
45. Sala dello Scudo
46. Sala Grimani
47. Sala Erizzo
48. Sala degli Stucchi
    or Priuli
49. Sala Dei Filosofi
50. Sala dei Leoni
51. Sala Corner

52. Sala dei Ritratti
53. Sala degli Scudieri
54. Sale del Magistrato
    alle Leggi
55. Sala della Quarantia
    Criminal

Liagò

Returning to the first floor
we come to the **Liagò**, the
chamber where nobles
gathered before and during
meetings of the Council.
It contains paintings by
Domenico Tintoretto, one
by Antonio Balestra, and one,
by Jacopo Palma il Giovane,
of *Doge Memmo Before the
Virgin with Patron Saints*
(dated 1615). The statues of
Adam and Eve, which used
to stand in the courtyard,
are by Antonio Rizzo.

Antonio Balestra,
Doge Giovanni Corner
Kneeling Before the
Virgin, *detail. Liagò.*

*Jacopo Palma
il Giovane,* Doge
Marcantonio Memmo
Before the Virgin with
Patron Saints. *Liagò.*

*View of the
Liagò.*

Sala della Quarantia Civil Vecchia

The **Sala della Quarantia Civil Vecchia** was the meeting-place for the forty members of the Quarantia Civile. This council, instituted in the 12th century, was divided in 1492 into two sections (Quarantia Vecchia and Quarantia Nuova), with different functions of the magistrature; in particular the Quarantia was responsible for passing sentence in serious criminal cases. The room's present appearance is due to a series of alterations in the course of the 17th century. On the walls are paintings by Pietro Malombra, *God the Father,* and *Venice Enthroned with the Virtues and Mercury Leading the Old and the Young Enchained,* a tabernacle with a 15th-century-panel of the *Madonna and Child*, and two canvases by Andrea Celesti depicting *Moses Destroying the Golden Calf* and *Moses Chastising the Jews for their Idolatry,* as well as a canvas representing *Venice among the Virtues Receiving the Sceptre of Power* by Giovan Battista Lorenzetti (1660); under the wooden dossals has been found an ancient fragment of painting in which the upper part of the Basilica of San Marco is still visible.

Quarantia Civil Vecchia, view.

Sala dell'Armamento

The **Sala dell'Armamento** (also known as the **Sala del Guariento**) was a store-room for weapons and munitions, and was originally connected to the Sala d'Armi and the Consiglio dei Dieci on the upper floors. At present it contains the remains of a fresco by Guariento, formerly in the Sala del Maggior Consiglio. Commissioned in about 1365, it represents the *Coronation of the Virgin*.

Badly damaged in the fire of 1577, it was then concealed behind the canvas of Tintoretto's *Paradise*; almost forgotten thereafter, it was only brought to light in the early years of the 20th century.

Guariento, fresco of the Coronation of the Virgin. *Sala dell'Armamento, or del Guariento.*

Sala del Maggior Consiglio

The **Sala del Maggior Consiglio** was the chamber where the most important legislative body of the Venetian state gathered to deliberate. The Maggior Consiglio or Grand Council was a very ancient body, comprising all noble Venetians above twenty years of age, whose mandate lasted one year (but they could stand for re-election). The assemblies were always presided over by the Doge and the Signoria. In 1297 the *Serrata* (or closure) of the Maggior Consiglio restricted the number of members and made them practically irremovable. Up to that time, the whole administration of the Venetian state had been effectively in the hands of the Maggior Consiglio; and even after it, when the legislative power had passed to the Senate, the Council still retained certain important prerogatives, such as the power to grant pardons. Its meetings were secret until the 16th century. The chamber was built in the mid-14th century, and the earliest paintings date from 1365. In that year Guariento, a Paduan artist, was commissioned to paint a fresco of the *Coronation of Maria* on the wall behind the throne. This fresco was badly

The **meetings of the Maggior Consiglio** were normally held on Sundays, and were preceded by the ringing of the bell of San Marco. The Signoria and the Dieci were responsible for ensuring that meetings were held behind closed doors and no weapons were brought into the chamber. The members, except for certain office-holders, would be seated in two rows, back-to-back. During the assemblies, armed guards were drawn up on both the Ponte della Paglia and in the Piazza, under the charge of the Procurators of San Marco, who waited under the loggia of the bell tower. It was in this chamber that the preliminary stages of the election of the Doge took place; voting would then be continued in the Sala dello Scrutinio. The election of a Doge was a particularly long and complicated procedure, in which voting alternated with the drawing of lots. A number of ballots,

damaged during the fire of 1577; it is now in the Sala del Guariento. In 1382 the Signoria urged the Procurators of San Marco to complete the decoration; towards the end of the 14th century they commissioned a number of painters to fresco the whole chamber; at the first sign of decay, these were replaced by paintings on canvas. It is likely, as Sansovino seems to suggest, that Guariento also painted other works that have not survived, and records show that the most celebrated painters of the day also worked in the chamber:

Gentile da Fabriano, Antonio Veneziano, Michelino da Besozzo, Alvise Vivarini, Jacobello del Fiore, Michele Giambono. The frescoes illustrated the history of relations between the Emperor and Pope, and the mediatory role of Venice, based on a set of inscriptions written by Petrarch during his stay in Venice (1362). It seems that these same inscriptions were also written on scrolls and displayed on the walls of the Grand Council hall. A document from 1425 not only cites the Petrarch texts, but comments on the imagery of the frescoes that accompanied

them, so it seems certain that they were finished by that date. In any case, we already know that under Doge Michele Steno (1400–1413) work was proceeding rapidly. There followed a period of stasis, due largely to the political and military difficulties of the Republic, and work was resumed only after 1470. It was decided not only to complete the gaps in the decoration, but also to renew the parts that had either decayed or failed to meet the changing taste of the day. The great fire of 1577 damaged both the wooden structures and the

corresponding to the number of nobles present, were placed in an urn; thirty of them were marked with the word "lector." Whoever received a ballot so marked remained in the chamber, the others left the room. The same

procedure was repeated to choose the electors, who in turn nominated forty "lectores"; then, by drawing lots, these were reduced to twelve, who elected twenty-five people and they, with a further ballot, were reduced to five. These

in turn had to elect forty-three people, reduced to eleven again by drawing lots. These eleven elected the forty-one electors of the Doge, who required a minimum of twenty-five votes to be elected.

Jacopo Tintoretto, Venice as Queen Offering an Olive Branch to Doge Nicolò da Ponte. *Sala del Maggior Consiglio, ceiling.*

View of the Sala del Maggior Consiglio.

*Paolo
Veronese,*
The Triumph
of Venice.
*Sala del Maggior
Consiglio, ceiling.*

*Jacopo
Palma
il Giovane,*
Venice Crowned
by Victory Triumphs
Over the Subject
Provinces.
*Sala del Maggior
Consiglio, ceiling.*

architecture of the Sala del Maggior Consiglio, while canvases and frescoes were almost completely destroyed. So extensive was the damage that the Signoria at first considered completely rebuilding the chamber. Finally partial reconstruction to a design by Antonio Rusconi was decided on; this retained the surviving features of the original, and the result is what one can see today. First it was decided to decorate the ceiling (by Cristoforo Sorte, 1582), and in 1587 a monk, Gerolamo Bardi, was commissioned to draft a detailed iconographic scheme, also based on the history of relations between Pope and Emperor, while adding episodes from the Fourth Crusade and other more strictly celebratory and symbolic themes. The central space was reserved for the glorification of the Republic. The design of the ceiling was conceived, in the taste of the period, as a sequence of large panels in which paintings on canvas were enclosed within sumptuous carved and gilded frames. There are three great paintings in the centre and twelve at the sides, while the spaces between the frames are filled with monochrome depictions of historical episodes or allegorical subjects. This imposing scheme was completed in the years of the dogeship of Nicolò da Ponte, and the most celebrated painters were, as usual, summoned to set their hands to the task. In 1579 Tintoretto and Veronese began work, followed by Jacopo Palma il Giovane and Francesco Bassano. The ceiling was completed by 1584, while the walls, begun in about 1590, were probably only completed early in the 17th century, except for Tintoretto's painting of *Paradise*, which took the artist from 1588 to 1594.

On the ceiling above the throne is Veronese's *Triumph of Venice*, a particularly rich

Tintoretto's painting of **Paradise** was originally executed on a smaller canvas for the Scuola Vecchia della Misericordia, and only later moved to the Sala del Maggior Consiglio, where it was finished in detail. A preparatory sketch for this splendid work is now in the Thyssen-Bornemisza Collection; it differs in some particulars from the finished painting.

Jacopo Tintoretto, Paradise, *sketch for the painting in the Sala del Maggior Consiglio. Madrid, Thyssen-Bornemisza Collection.*
This sketch was entered in the competition of 1588 but did not win:
the commission was only later assigned to Tintoretto after the death of Paolo Veronese, who had been originally chosen.

and spectacular work; while at the centre Jacopo Tintoretto (probably with assistants) depicted *Nicolò da Ponte Receiving the Laurel Crown from Venice* (1584). On the end wall is *Venice Crowned by Victory, which Receives the Subject Provinces,* by Jacopo Palma il Giovane: many preparatory studies for this work have been found. The twelve paintings at the sides of the ceiling (six per side) represent acts of heroism by the Republic's *condottieri* or episodes of war, such as the *Venetian Victory over the Milanese under Filippo Maria Visconti*, by Palma il Giovane, *Contarini's Conquest of Riva del Garda* by

Tintoretto and assistants, and the *Battle of Maclodio* by Francesco Bassano. Immediately below the ceiling there runs a frieze with portraits of the first sixty-six doges, from Obelerio Antenoreo to Francesco Venier (1554–1556). Most of these portraits are imaginary; the commission was given to Jacopo Tintoretto but they were mostly painted by his son Domenico. Each doge holds a scroll on which are illustrated the most important achievements of his reign. Of all the paintings on the walls the most impressive is probably Tintoretto's *Paradise*, commissioned in 1588. In painting this vast

Jacopo Tintoretto,
Victory of the Venetians
Over the Ferrarese
at Argenta. *Sala
del Maggior Consiglio,
ceiling.*

canvas, Tintoretto was assisted by his son Domenico. The work is richly imaginative in composition and the sense of movement given to each of the figures. The paintings on the wall towards the inner courtyard were executed later, in the late 16th and early 17th centuries, and represent (as said above) Venice's mediation between Papacy and Empire. Between one episode and another are represented certain symbols of authority carried by the doges in public processions (though their origin does not lie in papal grants, as the iconographic scheme suggests, but rather dates back to Byzantine times). The sequence of the twelve episodes starts with the painting of *Alexander III in Venice with Doge Ziani* by C. and G. Caliari, near the dais. The other historical cycle, running along the wall towards the quay, depicts episodes from the Fourth Crusade, which was of great importance for Venice's subsequent commercial expansion in the East. Among the canvases of this cycle are *Army of the Crusaders Besieges Zara* by Andrea Vicentino, the *Surrender of Zara* and the *Conquest of Constantinople* by Domenico Tintoretto, the *Crusaders Besieging Constantinople* by Jacopo Palma il Giovane. On the wall opposite the dais, in the centre, is *Doge Contarini Returning to Venice in Triumph after Defeating the Genoese*, by Paolo Veronese and assistants, commemorating the victory of 1379.

Domenico Tintoretto, Portrait of Giovanni Mocenigo. Sala del Maggior Consiglio, frieze.

Domenico Tintoretto, Portrait of Mario Barbarigo. Sala del Maggior Consiglio, frieze.

A typical instance of *damnatio memoriae* can be seen in the frieze of the Doges of Venice. Doge Marin Faliero (1354-1355) was accused of conspiracy against the state and beheaded. In the panel where his portrait should appear there is a black curtain with this inscription: HIC EST LOCUS MARINI FALETHRI DECAPITATI PRO CRIMINIBUS (this is the place of Marin Faliero, beheaded for his crimes).

From the Sala della Quarantia Civil Nuova to the Sala del Magistrato alle Leggi I

Next to the Sala del Maggior Consiglio is the **Sala della Quarantia Civil Nuova,** the council chamber for the magistrature instituted in 1492, which dealt with cases in the provinces subject to Venice. The chamber, restructured after 1577, contains paintings alluding to the functions of the magistracy, by artists of the early 17th century. The **Sala dello Scrutinio,** also restored in 1579–1599 after being damaged by fire, was where

Sala della Quarantia Civil Nuova, view.

Andrea Vicentino,
The Battle of Lepanto.
Sala dello Scrutinio.

Antonio Vassillachi,
Clemency. *Sala dello Scrutinio, ceiling.*

and assistants; the others, which continue the series down to Doge Ludovico Manin (1789–1797) were the work of artists contemporary with the doges themselves. On the wall behind the dais is the very fine *Last Judgment* by Palma il Giovane (1594–1595: note the arms of Doge Francesco Foscari), which replaced Tintoretto's painting of the same subject, lost in the fire. On the end wall, towards the Scala Foscari, is the monument to Francesco Morosini (c. 1694) designed by A. Gaspari, with paintings by Lazzarini representing the achievements of this Venetian *condottiero*. The **Sala della Quarantia Criminal** is decorated with 17th-century stalls, while the walls of the **Sala del Magistrato alle Leggi I** display paintings by Flemish artists: *Paradise*, the *Fall of the Damned*, *Empyrean*, *Inferno*, the *Triptych of the Hermits* and the *Triptych of the Martyrdom of St. Liberata* by Hieronymus Bosch, and *Christ Mocked* by Quentin Metsys.

voting took place for elections to the various offices of state. A previous ceiling dated from the 1630s and was the work of Serlio, with paintings by Pordenone; the present one is by Sorte, with a series of carved and gilded mouldings. The scheme of decoration, devised by the monk Gerolamo de' Bardi, envisaged thirty-nine painted panels depicting naval victories by the Venetians in the East and the conquest of Padua. Nearly all the paintings were commissioned from Tintoretto and Veronese and their pupils. Changes were made to the program, so that some paintings were added in the following century. The frieze repeats the motif of the portraits of doges (as in the Sala del Maggior Consiglio): the earliest were by Tintoretto

Hieronymus Bosch,
Paradise and Empyrean.
Sala del Magistrato
alle Leggi I.

Hieronymus Bosch,
Triptych of the Hermits,
detail. Sala del
Magistrato alle Leggi I.

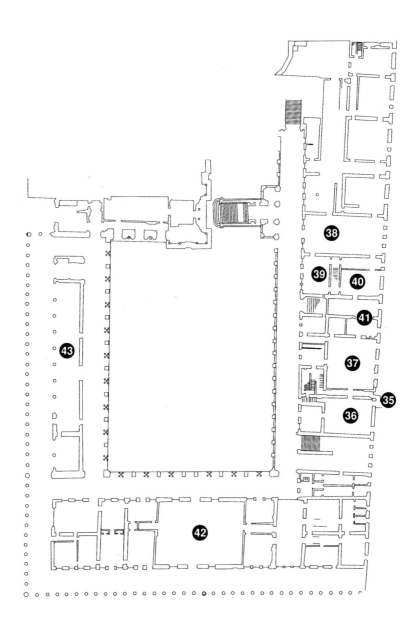

Plan of the loggias.
35. Bridge of Sighs
36. Sala dei Censori
37. Sala dell'Avogadria
38. Cancelleria Inferiore
39. Sala della Bolla
40. Sala della Milizia da Mar
41. Sala dello Scrigno
42. Sala del Piovega
43. Loggia Foscara

Bridge of Sighs

A corridor leads on to the celebrated **Bridge of Sighs**, initially designed by Rusconi, continued by Da Ponte and completed by Antonio and Tommaso Contino (1614). The bridge was built to join the Doge's Palace with the newly-built **Prigioni Nuove** alongside. It is closed and roofed over: the decoration of the exterior foreshadows the Baroque style and it is decorated with bas-reliefs of *Justice* and the arms of the Doge Marino Grimani (1595–1606). The name is a 19th century literary invention. The Prigioni Nuove were designed by Da Ponte but constructed by Antonio Contin, who completed them in the early 17th century.

The Bridge of Sighs.

From the Sala dei Censori to the Sala della Bolla

Returning to the Doge's Palace, we enter the **Sala dei Censori**, where a frieze presents the portraits of magistrates by Domenico Tintoretto.
The **Sala dell'Avogadria** was the council chamber for a very ancient magistracy, made up of three members (or *"Avogadri"*) elected by the Maggior Consiglio; it dealt with fiscal problems and acted as public prosecutor in trials, with the principal task of ensuring application of the laws. On the wall by the entrance is a *Resurrection with Three*

Avogadri by Domenico Tintoretto and the *Madonna in Glory with Three Avogadri* by Leandro Bassano. Other paintings by D. Tintoretto are on the wall opposite the windows.
In the **Sala dello Scrigno** there is an 18th-century cabinet containing the *Libro d'Oro*, in which all the nobility were enrolled, and the *Libro d'Argento*, which listed the citizenry. The walls are decorated with portraits of Avogadri and Censors, notable among which are the *Portrait of Three*

Avogadori by Pietro Uberti and the *Virgin in Glory and Child with Three Avogadri* by Nicolà Renieri. The **Sala della Milizia da Mar**, housed the meeting place for the *Zonta* whose task was to keep the galleys fitted out and properly manned, contains original Cinquecento furnishings and paintings by the school of Tiepolo.
The **Sala della Bolla** was the chamber of the official who approved official transactions; it, too, is decorated with portraits of Avogadri and Censors.

Domenico Tintoretto, Annunciation and Portraits of Three Avogadri. Sala dei Censori.

View of the Sala dei Censori.

Domenico Tintoretto, Resurrection and Three Avogadri. *Sala dell'Avogadria.*

Pietro Uberti, Portraits of Three Avogadri. *Sala dello Scrigno.*

Cortile dei Senatori, Porticato and Arco Foscari, Scala dei Giganti

Passing through the loggia, we descend to the floor below and emerge into the **Cortile dei Senatori**, probably a gathering place for senators before the assemblies began. The façade was built in the early 16th century and is attributed to Giorgio Spavento; in imitation of Rizzo's design for the façade alongside; the upper storey is lightened by a row of windows with columns and tympana, decorated in polychrome marble. Opposite stands the **Porticato Foscari** (1440–1450) which, in ancient times—even before the year 1000—was the only fortified entrance to the castle. At the head of the portico, on the opposite side the Porta della Carta, is the **Arco Foscari**, begun in the 1460s, still with a Gothic flavour but with Renaissance ornaments. At the top are a series of pinnacles with statues of *St. Mark and the Liberal Arts* by Bregno and Rizzo. The **Sala dei Giganti** was designed by Antonio Rizzo in 1483-1485, and the sculptures were completed by 1491. The name comes from the two stone statues of *Mars* and *Neptune* carved by Jacopo Sansovino

and set on the upper parapet in 1567. The structure is dressed with marble and decorated with bas-reliefs in full Renaissance style. Some rooms of the Doge's Palace can be seen only by guided parties, called "segret itineraries." It is possible to visit the offices and Sala della Cancelleria, which used to contain the most reserved

documents, the secret passage leading to the Sala del Consiglio dei Dieci, the Sala dei Tre Capi and the Sala degli Inquisitori, whose ceiling is decorated with canvases by Tintoretto (c. 1556) depicting the *Return of the Prodigal Son Surrounded by Four Virtues.* Other rooms that can be visited are the Torture Chamber, the prisons under the leads, known as "I Piombi," where Giacomo Casanova was imprisoned, and the kitchens of the palace in the depths of the building.

Scala dei Giganti, detail of the reliefs on the sides of the staircase.

Antonio Rizzo,
of Adam *and* Eve. Liagò.
The statues were
originally installed
in the niches of the Arco
Foscari, but today they
have been substituted
by bronze copies.

The Scala dei Giganti.

Jacopo Sansovino,
Mars *and* Neptune.
Scala dei Giganti.

Museo Correr

The Ala Napoleonica of Piazza San Marco and the Procuratie Nuove are now the premises of the Museo Correr. This important collection illustrates the civic and cultural heritage of Venice; its name commemorates Teodoro Correr (1750–1830), who founded the collection. A dedicated collector, on his death this Venetian nobleman left thousands of objects and paintings which formed the core of the present holdings of the civic museums. The collection, first opened to the public in 1836, used to be housed in the Correr family's palace on the Grand Canal at San Zandegolà. Subsequent donations and acquisitions enlarged the collection until it had to be moved to the Fondaco dei Turchi, in a nearby palace specially fitted out as a museum and opened in 1887. The principle underlying the new layout was to document Venetian history and civilisation; so it was divided into sections, each dealing with an aspect of Venetian social life in the 16th and 17th centuries. This arrangement remains substantially unchanged today. In 1922 the museum moved to its present premises in the Procuratie Nuove, with access from the large staircase of the Ala Napoleonica on the piazza. Some sections of the civic museums have now been relocated to create collections which have premises of their own but are still part of the civic heritage. An example is Correr's collection of 18th-century paintings which, together with later acquisitions, have been on display since 1936 in the splendid setting of Ca' Rezzonico, while 19th-century paintings are held in the gallery of modern art in Ca' Pesaro. Since 1953 the Casa Goldoni in San Polo has housed a library, archives, and other facilities. It has recently been decided to bring together the rich collection of textiles in Ca' Mocenigo at San Stae to create a centre for studies in the history of Textiles and Costume. The idea of screening off the side of the piazza facing the Basilica of San Marco by building the Palazzo Reale arose under the French Kingdom of Italy (1807). There was a pressing need for a large building whose central features would be the Ballroom and a splendid staircase. The architect of the new building was Giuseppe Soli, but the design was altered, and it was only constructed in 1830–1840. The museum occupies most of the rooms of the ancient Palace and is divided into a number of sections. The fine Neo-Classical interiors of the first-floor make an ideal setting for the works of Antonio Canova. Three of these rooms have been open to the public since June 1996. The first floor also contains the historical section of the museum; particularly interesting is the section devoted to cartography, a science which reached remarkable heights at quite an early date in representations of Venice. There are rooms devoted to Crafts and Trades, Games and Festivals, with the aim of representing aspects of everyday life in the past, so reflecting the interests of the

Giovanni Bellini,
Dead Christ Supported
by Two Angels, *detail.*

museum's founder. The first floor also has a rich collection of bronzes (recently enlarged). The second floor contains the splendid picture gallery, with important masterpieces of Venetian art from the origins down to the Renaissance; and there is a museum devoted to the Risorgimento period.

The present design of the installation is by the architect Carlo Scarpa, who worked on it in two periods, 1952–1953 and 1960, when the picture gallery was laid out. The Museo del Risorgimento was designed by the City of Venice's art department in 1980. The rooms devoted to Arts and Trades and Games date from 1993.

Between 1806 and 1814, under the Kingdom of Italy created by Napoleon, Venice was second only to Milan in importance and it therefore required a royal palace and public state rooms.

Eugène Beauharnais ordered a sumptuous staircase to be built on the site of the church of San Geminiano, a fine building by Jacopo Sansovino. The architects chosen were Giuseppe Soli and Lorenzo Santi. The present *Glory of Neptune* frescoed on the ceiling by

Piazza San Marco, View of the Procuratie Nuove and the Ala Napoleonica which now houses the Museo Correr.

Vogel-Richter, View of Piazza San Marco Towards the Ancient Church of San Geminiano, *engraving.*

Sebastiano Santi dates from 1837–1838, when the palace was largely restructured.

The staircase leads to the ante-room, with the ticket office, wardrobe and bookshop, and leads into the exhibition area.

Bernardino Castelli, Portrait of Teodoro Correr, *founder of the collection.*

Monumental staircase in the Palazzo Reale giving access to the museum.

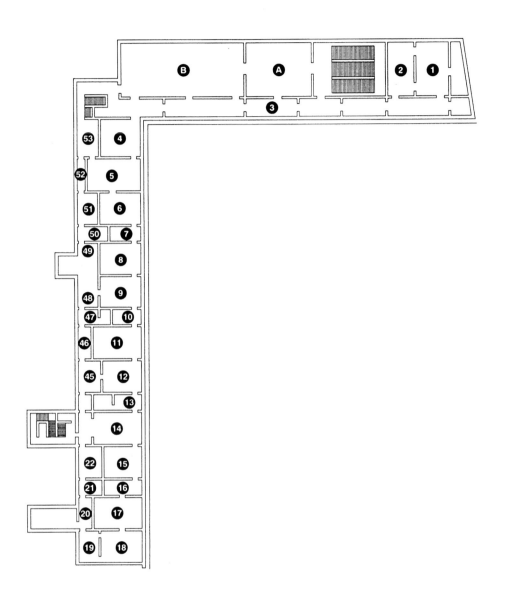

Plan of the
Museo Corror
First floor.
A. Antechamber-Ticket
    Office-Bookshop-
    Wardrobe
B Ballroom
1. Exhibition room
    and Cafeteria
2. Fine Arts room

3. Canova's Gallery
4. Throne Room
5. Dining Room
6–18. Venetian Civilization
19–22. Miniature Bronzes
45–53. Venetian Civilization

Room 1 and Room of the Fine Arts

The **first floor** is laid out in three large sections: Rooms 1–5 are devoted to Canova; 6–18 and 45–53 to Venetian life and culture; 19–22 to bronzes. **Room 1** is to the left of the visitor and decorated with floral motifs. Between the two windows is the Portrait of Teodoro Correr by Bernardino Castelli, known to have been painted before 1795, when an engraving was made from it. Further on is the **Room of the Fine Arts**, frescoed, like many other interiors of the palace, by Giuseppe Borsato. Figures, in perfect Empire style, are by Piero Moro. The spaces beyond are used for temporary exhibitions and at the far end is a coffee shop. The core of the rooms which are devoted to the celebrated Venetian sculptor Antonio Canova (Canova's Gallery, Throne Room, Dining Room and Ballroom) constituted the principal state rooms of the Palazzo Reale built from 1804 onwards and restructured in 1835-1840.

Pietro Moro and Giuseppe Borsato, wall decorations in the Fine Arts room.

Canova's Gallery

Entering the **Canova's Gallery** (also called the **Loggia Napoleonica**), which runs along the shorter side of Piazza San Marco opposite the basilica, one sees Canova's *Self-Portrait*, a plaster of Paris cast of the sculpture carved in 1812 and kept at Possagno.

Along the walls are numerous works cast in plaster of Paris and never carved in marble. They represent episodes from the Homeric poems and Plato's *Phaedo* (they date from some time between 1787 and 1792). Two represent *Works of Mercy*. On the left, as you enter, there is the *Death of Priam*, the mythical king of Troy, and to the right the *Dance of the Sons of Alcinous*; further on (right) are the *Trojans Offering the Peplum to Paris, Breiseis Consigned to the Heralds* and the *Return of Telemachus to Ithaca*. On the left the subjects

are *Feed the Hungry* and *Teach the Ignorant*. These last two reliefs (the second is signed and dated 1796) represent two of the seven Works of Mercy; they were probably commissioned by Senator Abbondio Rezzonico of Rome, to adorn a free school which the nobleman had founded near Bassano. The *Fruit Baskets*, dated 1774, displayed at the end of this part of the loggia, were carved for the balustrade of the palace of Daniele Farsetti at San

Lucas; they are thus among Canova's earliest works. Continuing along the gallery we come, on the right, to a preparatory study for the *Monument to Titian*, and on the left the *Herm* of the *Vestal Tuccia* and the *Herm* of *Sappho*. These last two works in plaster of Paris were given by Canova to the daughter of Doge Paolo Renier.

Room 3: the gallery closes with the fine cast of *Paris*, with carved on the trunk the date 12 May 1807. This cast, with the holes of the mould still visible, illustrates the process by which the marble statues were made from the cast. The *Paris* was donated to the museum by the Falier family, which had received it from Canova himself; two marble versions of it exist, one carved for Josephine Beauharnais (1807–1812) and the other for Louis of Bavaria (1810–1816).

Antonio Canova,
Feed the Hungry,
plaster bas-relief.

Antonio Canova ,
Death of Priam,
plaster bas-relief.

Antonio Canova,
Monument to Titian,
maquette.

Ballroom, Throne Room and Dining Room

Next to Room 3 is the **Ballroom**. This splendid interior was designed by the architect Lorenzo Santi, beginning in 1822. Work and alterations went on for a long time, and it was only completed twenty years later, in 1843. The spacious rectangular chamber ends and is enhanced by the loggia for the orchestra, whose curved and gilded balustrades create

the illusion that the room is actually oval. The decorations are by Giuseppe Borsato. This room contains the group of *Orpheus and Eurydice*, carved by Canova in Vicenza stone. It is an early work which was exhibited at the Fiera dell'Ascensione in 1777 and placed in the garden of Villa Falier at Asolo. The artist carved the figures at two different times, *Eurydice*

being the earlier. Along the edge of the pedestal runs an inscription with verses of Virgil and Ovid alluding to the myth of Orpheus, who descended into Hades to recover his bride Eurydice, charming the terrible guardians of the underworld with his music. His wish was granted, provided he did not turn to look at her before they were safely above the ground;

Francesco Hayez,
Thetys Immerses
Achilles in the Waters
of Styx, *detached fresco.*
Throne Room.

Francesco Hayez,
Mercury Gives Paris
the Apple of Discord,
detached fresco.
Throne Room.

Antonio Canova,
Orpheus and Eurydice,
1777. Ballroom.

but overcome by desire he
failed to keep the pact and she
was lost to him.

At the end of the Ballroom
there is an ante-chamber with
bas-reliefs similar to those in
the gallery. They represent
three episodes from Plato's
Phaedo: from left to right,
*Socrates Leaves His
Family*, *Socrates Drinks
the Hemlock*, and *Criton
Closes Socrates' Eyes*. On the
left are displayed two *Virtues*:
Charity and *Hope*.

Further on we come to
what was once the
Throne Room (Room 4),
decorated with frescoes by
Giuseppe Borsato, while the
lunettes with a gold ground
are by Giovanni Battista Canal
(c. 1811–1813). The frescoes
on the walls have been
removed and transferred to
canvas. They were part of the
original decoration of the
palace. Those by Francesco
Hayez (1817) are in the Sala
del Generale Consiglio
(Procuratie Nuove), while the
charming *Four Seasons* by
Giovanni Carlo Bevilacqua
(1813) are still on the wall
opposite the windows. Also by
Bevilacqua is the allegorical
fresco of *Victory Leading
Faith to Crown Europe* (1814).
Framed by stucco decorations,
Hayez's paintings were
removed in 1950. The
monochrome medallions depict
episodes from the *Iliad*:
Thetys Receives the Arms

Antonio Canova,
Daedalus and Icarus,
1778–1779.
Throne Room.

of *Achilles from Vulcan*, and *Jove and Juno*; above the door are *Mercury Gives Paris the Apple of Discord*, and *Thetys Immerses Achilles in the Waters of Styx*. Below the monochrome medallions are compartments with elegant *Dancers*. Between the windows is the cast of *Winged Cupid* which Canova carved for the Russian Prince Yusupov in 1793–1797. At the centre of the room stands the splendid group of *Daedalus and Icarus* from the Palazzo Pisani in Venice.

Room 5 was formerly the dining-room of the palace and is one of its best-preserved Neo-Classical interiors. The rich decoration is by Giuseppe Borsato. Particularly noteworthy are the charming *Views* set in the tondos between the wall decorations. Venice, in the tondo on the left of the entrance, is represented by Piazza San Marco during a flood. These landscapes gave the room one of its names, *Sala dei Paesaggi*. The ceiling fresco by Giovanni Carlo Bevilacqua depicts *Olympus*. On the easel are two paintings by Canova: on the right, the uncompleted *Portrait of Amadeo Svajer* and to the left is *Cupid and Psyche*. The Neo-Classical table in the centre of the room is a very fine piece: the top in white and blue Sèvres porcelain is decorated with mythological

and allegorical scenes. A similar table, once owned by Josephine Beauharnais, is at Malmaison. Between the windows is a plaster of Paris cast of the *Italian Venus*.

Daedalus and Icarus were commissioned by the Procurator Pietro Vettor Pisani, whose daughters later donated it to the city of Venice. It is a youthful work. The two protagonists of the tragic myth related by Ovid are delicately depicted at one of the most melancholy moments: when the aged Daedalus applies the waxen wings to the shoulders of Icarus, unmindful of his tragic end. Seized by enthusiasm for flight, the youth soars too near the sun, which melts the waxen wings. At the feet of the figures Canova represented the tools used to carve marble, a detail justified by Daedalus's craft, but also an allusion to Sculpture, of which this statue is such a splendid allegory.

Antonio Canova, Portrait of the Celebrated Antiquary Amedeo Svajer. *Dining Room.*

Rooms 6–7

Room 6 begins the display of objects illustrating Venetian life and culture. The theme of this and the next room is the figure of the **doge**, the highest office of the Venetian magistracy. Of remote origins, the powers of the holder of this office changed through the centuries; but he had always to be of patrician rank and his appointment was for life. Of great interest in this first room are the two paintings on the wall to the right of the entrance, originally organ doors from the church of San Michele in Isola. Painted by the Brescian artists Giovanni and Bernardino da Asola in 1526, they represent (left) *St. Benedict and Two Monks* and (right) *Doge Pietro Orseolo Before St. Romualdo*. Pietro Orseolo abandoned the dogeship to become a Benedictine monk in an abbey in the Pyrenees, where he died in 987. On the wall by the entrance hangs the great canvas of Aliense (Antonio Vassilacchi) depicting the *Arrival of Queen Caterina Cornaro of Cyprus* which took place in 1489. The painting is from the Doge's Palace. Opposite is a painting by Andrea Michiel, in the same format, of the *Arrival of the Dogaressa Morosina Morosini*

Grimani at the Doge's Palace, an event that took place in 1597. Another poetic episode in the life of the doges is recounted in the painting between the windows by Gian Antonio Guardi; it is a replica of the painting by Paris Bordone for the Scuola Grande di San Marco (now in the Gallerie dell'Accademia). This is the *Presentation of the Ring to the Doge:* a fisherman gives the doge the ring received from St. Mark. Note the very fine *Portrait of Francesco Foscari* by Lazzaro Bastiani (c. 1460): the doge and *condottiero* is represented with all the honours of his office. The display cases contain precious objects also associated with the office. Of particular note is the fragment of a tapestry displayed between the showcases, with its outstanding *Portrait of Doge Lorenzo Grimani* (or Leonardo Loredan), part of the altarpiece that was traditionally presented to the basilica of San Marco after the doge took the oath of office. **Room 7** is devoted more specifically to the solemn moment of the **doge's election** and the civic festivities he presided over. The electoral system was highly complicated so as to avoid irregularities, as

is shown by the objects in the display cabinet on the right. On the left wall is a woodcut by Matteo Pagan (1559), illustrating one of the most significant public events in the doge's life: the *Doge's Procession to Piazza San Marco*. The painting by Heintz on the left wall illustrates the *Procession for the Feast of the Redeemer:* the doge would go every year with a procession of boats to the church of the Redentore to give thanks for the end of the terrible plague of 1576.

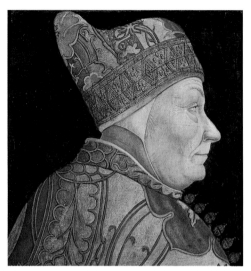

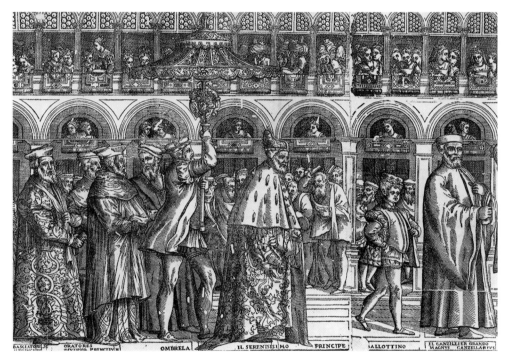

Lazzaro Bastiani, Portrait of Doge Francesco Foscari. *Sala del Doge.*

Portrait of Doge Lorenzo Grimani (or Leonardo Loredan), *fragment of a tapestry.* *Sala del Doge.*

Matteo Pagano, Doge's Procession in Piazza San Marco, *engraving, detail.* *Sala dell'elezione del Doge.*

Room 8

The very fine **bookcases** in **Room** 8 are from the convent of San Nicola da Tolentino, of the Theatine Order, which was suppressed in the Napoleonic period. The furnishings were then moved to Palazzo Pisani. They include 17th century inlaid furniture in solid walnut which contain manuscripts and fine books from the 16th and 17th centuries and the doge's Commissions which are a feature of the museum. The showcases at the centre of the room contain books with fine silver and leather bindings. The 18th-century chandelier is particularly beautiful; like that in the following chamber it was produced by the Murano glassworks of Giuseppe Briati. After the doge, the major officers in the Venetian magistracy were the senators and procurators. The latter supervised and administered the Basilica of San Marco, and gave their name to the range of buildings—the Procuratie—facing the square, where they used to meet.

Teatini Library.
The 18th-century chandelier
was produced by Giuseppe
Briati's workshop
on Murano.

Rooms 9–12

Room 9 and **Room 10**
(Sale delle Magistrature) are
the portraits of some of these
magistrates, originally in
Palazzo Morosini. The
Procurators can be recognised
by the velvet stole covering
their shoulders. In **Room 10**
there is a very fine *Portrait
of Vincenzo Querini* by the
painter Bartolomeo Nazari
of Bergamo (18th century).
Over the door of the previous
chamber, there is the equally
interesting *Portrait of Pietro
Balbi,* from the Cinquecento
Veneto school.
The museum's rich collection
of medals is partly displayed
in cabinets in **Room 11**
(Numismatics). Of great
interest is the complete series
of coins struck by the Venetian
Republic. A curiosity is the
collection of "Oselle" in the
cabinet on the right. These
were gold and silver medals,
often current coin, which were
issued to commemorate the
gift of birds made by the doge
every New Year to the
Venetian patricians. The
finances of the state were
under the charge of three
functionaries called
"Camerlenghi." We see them
depicted in the fine canvas by
Jacopo Tintoretto (on the wall
by the entrance to the room):
the subject of the painting is

Batolomeo Nazari,
Portrait of Doge Vincenzo
Querini.
Sala delle Magistrature.

St. Justine in the act of
protecting these three
functionaries, identified as
Marco Giustiniani, Angelo
Morosini and Alessandro
Badoer. The painting was
originally in the Palazzo dei
Camerlenghi on Rialto. On the
left-hand wall hangs an
enormous naval ensign with
the arms of Doge Domenico
Contarini.

The sea was all-important in
the history of Venice. The
city's fleet, the instrument of
defence and dominion, was the
source of its political and
commercial power. In the
middle of **Room 12 (Venice
and the sea)** can be seen two
models of galleys, the swift
craft designed for war and the
defence of the lagoon, and also
for the escort of merchant
ships. A collection of the very
fine lamps hung on the galleys
are also displayed at the
centre of the room. The
cabinets contain instruments
of navigation. On the end wall
hang two canvases by an
anonymous 16th century
Venetian painter depicting
episodes from the battle of
Lepanto (1571), where Venice
defeated the Turks. The side
walls have 17th-century
paintings showing the battle
array of the Turkish and
Venetian fleets.

*16th century Veneto
school,* Battle of Lepanto,
*room dedicated to Venice
and the sea.*

Jacopo Tintoretto,
St. Justine and the
Treasurers. *Room
devoted to Numismatics.*

Antonio di Natale,
Plan of the Arsenal,
*water-colour.
Sala dell'Arsenal.*

Rooms 13–14

Room 13 is devoted to the **Arsenal**, the shipyards where the naval fleet and, in some cases, merchant ships were fitted out. Very rare and of the greatest interest is the 18th-century water-colour of the *Plan of the Arsenal* by Antonio di Natale (left wall); it was unusual for the Arsenal to be painted because of the secrecy shrouding the construction of warships. Also noteworthy is the *Portrait of Angelo Memmo IV in the Uniform of Admiral of the Fleet* by Alessandro Longhi. It depicts clearly the red damask with gold brocade of the costume worn by the commander of the fleet. Quite accurate depictions of the city of Venice are common from early times. The

collection of plans in **Room 14** (**Venezia Forma Urbis**) are thus of great interest, starting from the celebrated 16th-century engraving of the plan of Venice by Jacopo de Barbari; the gigantic plate from which it was taken is also displayed. On the wall opposite are hung paintings that illustrate the changes to the 16th-century plan through the centuries: there is a late 16th- or early-17th-century canvas by Giovan Battista Arzenti and a mid-17th-century view in perspective by Giovan Battista Heintz. On the end wall hangs the symbol of Venice, the Lion of St. Mark, a 17th century wooden sculpture from the chancel of the basilica of San Marco. Opposite is the plaque

known as the *Edict of Egnazio*: it was carved by the humanist Giovan Battista Cipelli and comes from the headquarters of the Magistrato alle Acque, which supervised the security of the waters of the lagoon; it is a solemn admonition to whoever might threaten the peace of the Republic by sea. The central space is occupied by two large globes by the Venetian cartographer Vincenzo Coronelli (1650–1718): they represent the celestial globe and the earth.

Rooms 15–18

Next follow **Room 15** and **Room 16 (Correr Armoury)**. They are devoted to Venice's military power. The weapons on display, Italian and European, come from the collection by Teodoro Correr. Room 15 contains armour from the 15th and 16th centuries. Note (first on the left) the ship-armour with Nuremberg punch-work. The fire-arms and cutting weapons date from the 14th, 15th and 17th centuries. On the end wall hangs a Turkish fabric with an inscription from the Koran in Arabic script. The next room contains fire-arms, including a ship's cannon with twelve mouths, called an "Organo" (17th century). Also interesting are some of the pistols in the display cases, including one from a Brescian workshop, bearing the maker's name, LAZARINO COMINAZO, on the barrel (c. 1670).
The museum has a wealth of items related to the exploits of Francesco Morosini, the celebrated condottiero nicknamed "il Peleponnesiaco" or conqueror of the Peleponnese. They were acquired in 1895 and transferred to the Civic Collections from the palace of the Morosini family at Santo Stefano; now they are partly

collected in **Room 17** (Sala Morosini). Morosini won a number of victories against the Turks and was also celebrated for his conquest of Athens (during which he destroyed the Parthenon). Elected doge in 1688, he died in battle in 1694 during one of his campaigns against the Turks. On the right of the room as one enters there are cannons of various sizes, for use on galleys, and 17th-century harquebuses. The arms of the family, carved in wood, hang from the wall. On the left of the entrance is a set of six paintings of the 17th century Venetian school which illustrate episodes in Morosini's life. Between the windows is the imposing triple ship's lamp that hung on the poop of Morosini's galley in his last campaign against the Turks. Other objects belonging to the doge are on display, including a prayer-book and prie-dieu from his flagship. Also note two paintings by Gregorio Lazzarini, replicas of those on the Arco Morosini in the Doge's Palace celebrating the condottiero.
Room 18 (Morosini Armoury) contains trophies and plunder won by Francesco Morosini. On the wall hangs a Portrait of the Doge on Horseback by Giovanni

Carboncino dating from 1688, the year of his election. The cabinets contain 17th century Oriental (right) and Venetian weapons (left).The shields on the walls are part of the Morosini war booty taken from the Turks.

17th century Veneto school, Portrait of Doge Francesco Morosini. *Sala Morosini.*

View of the Correr Armoury.

Alessandro Piazza, Francesco Morosini Leaving St. Mark's Basin for the Levant. *Sala Morosini.*

Rooms 19–22

Rooms 19-20-21-22 display part of the museum's rich collection of **miniature bronzes**. Bronzes were a form of art that had their heyday in the Renaissance; Cinquecento bronzes of this kind are mostly copies of celebrated masterpieces of Classical art on a reduced scale and hence easy to handle. They were so popular that they became an independent form of art and often reached surprising artistic heights. In Northern Italy, Padua and Venice were especially renowned for their bronzes.

In Venice two illustrious sculptors, Tullio and Antonio Lombardo, were outstanding in this field.

In **Room 19** the cabinet against the left-hand wall contains examples of their work. Note the *Venus with a Diadem* and the *Bust of a Woman.* Padua, with the spectacular altar by Donatello in the Basilica of Sant'Antonio and a proud antiquarian tradition, was inevitably a leader in popularising this art form and raising it to levels of great refinement. It was, in fact, a pupil of Donatello, Bartolomeo Bellano, who commenced production of

such bronzes in Padua. But it was above all Andrea Briosco, known as Riccio (1470/75–1532), who was the supreme master of the art and created a flourishing workshop. He also revealed the practical qualities of such bronzes, which could be adapted to the most varied domestic uses—ink-pots, lamp-holders, etc. His objects also intrigue by their naturalism, which combines myth and fantasy and makes them very differ-ent from his other, more monumental and classical sculptures. These bronzes diverge widely from the dictates of Reniassance art, with its emphasis on an Apollonian classicism, and seem to draw on the Dionysian and popular spirit which also pervades primitive mediaeval sculpture. Miniature bronzes from the workshops of Riccio and Severo da Ravenna are displayed in the cabinets in Room 19. **Room 20** is devoted to **Utensils**, in which the workshops of Alberghetti and that of Giuseppe di Levi from Verona dominated the Venetian market. They include bells with handles of various forms, ink-pots and mortars. The next room **(Room 21)** exhibits the work of two great 16th-century architects and sculptors: Jacopo Sansovino and Alessandro Vittoria. Sansovino came to Venice from Florence, where he had made his name as a sculptor, and influenced the leading sculptor of the Venetian Cinquecento, Alessandro Vittoria (1552–1608). These display cases contain splendid bronzes,

Workshop of Severo da Ravenna (attributed to), David with the Head of Goliath. *Room 19.*

pervaded by an intense dynamism which foreshadows the Baroque and is very evident in the door-knockers; note that of *Neptune and Sea-Horses* in the central cabinet. **Room 22** has some fine items from the two great Venetian workshops active in the late 16th and early 17th centuries: the *bottega* of Tiziano Aspetti (1556–1607) and Niccolò Roccatagliata (active c. 1539–1636) produced the very fine *Bacchus Pouring Wine* in the central case; from that of Gerolamo Campagna (died 1626) comes the set of angels from the Venetian church of San Lorenzo, dating from 1615–1618.

From Room 22 we can take the staircase that leads to the Pinacoteca (Art Gallery) and the Museo Risorgimentale on the second floor; or else continue the tour of the rooms devoted to Venetian life and culture on the first floor.

Gerolamo Campagna,
Salt-cellar in the form
of Neptune holding
a sea-shell. Room 20.

Alessandro Vittoria,
doorknocker with
Neptune and sea-horses.
Room 21.

Paduan workshop (?),
early 16th century,
Boy Taking a Thorn
from His Foot.
Room 19.

Rooms 45–53

Room 45 focuses on the **Bucintoro**, the splendid state barge on board of which the doges celebrated the ritual betrothal with the sea. Each year on the Feast of the Ascension, the state barge was sailed to the Lido for the traditional rite. Already in use in the 14th century, the Bucintoro seems to have even more ancient origins. The last of these barges was built in 1722–1728, carved and gilded by Antonio Corradini. All that remains of it is the splendid hatch cover here on display, depicting *St. Mark*, the city's patron saint. Through this aperture the doge would cast the ring that wedded Venice to the sea.

Room 46 (Festivals). Festivals were the high points of the relationship between the city and its citizens. The three paintings by the 17th-century artist Heintz the Younger depict three of the many traditional festivities in the Venetian calendar: the *Entrance of the Patriarch Federico Corner to San Pietro di Castello*, with boats adorned for Carnival, the *Bull Chase in Campo San Paolo*, presented for the doge by the company of Becheri (butchers), and the *Boat Trip to Murano*.

Room 47 is a small room with three important paintings, including the *Family Portrait* attributed to Cesare Vecellio.

Rooms 48–51 are devoted to **Arts and Trades**. Venice was not, of course, the only city to have trade guilds in which all citizens and foreigners who practised the same calling were invited to enrol. In Venice each of these "Arti" had its own rules, known as *mariegole*. All the Venetian guilds came under the "Magistratura della Giustizia Vecchia," with its headquarters in the Palazzo dei Camerlenghi. The signs of the guilds in this room come from this palace and were probably used to display notices about the guilds' rules, fees and and guild activities. In the 16th and 17th centuries they were made of wood, with the arms of the Magistratura della Giustizia Vecchia, the lion of St. Mark and the guild's patron saint, to whom an altar would be dedicated in one of the churches. **Room 50** is wholly devoted to the **Arte dei Dipintori** (painters' guild),

and contains the artistic 18th-century sign with *St. Lucy*, while **Room 51** is devoted to the **Arte dei Tagliapietra** (masons). Another interesting chapter of Venetian life was the city's **games**, documented in **Rooms 52–53**: they bring out, among other things, a rather cynical and disenchanted side of Venice. Gambling became socially acceptable as early as the start of the 17th century, with special premises established for it in 1638: the foyer of Palazzo Dandolo at San Moisè. This was the city's first public *casino*. The pictures in Room 52 illustrate the *Forze d'Ercole*, acrobatic displays popular at festivities.

18th century Veneto school, Sign of a Guild. Sala delle Arti e dei Mestieri.

Antonio Corradini, Hatch-cover of the Doge's barge. Sala del Bucintoro.

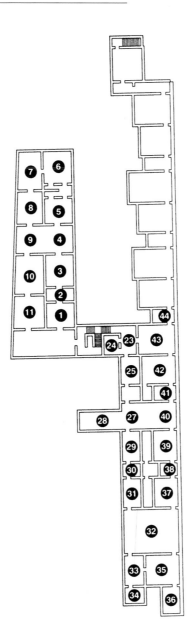

Plan of the Museo Correr
Second floor.
24. Veneto-Byzantine
    painters.
25. Paolo Veneziano
26. Lorenzo Veneziano
27. Decorated Gothic
29. International Gothic
30. Cosmè Tura
31.1. The Ferrarese

31.2. Vivarini, Boldrini
32. Sala delle Quattro
    Porte
33. Flemish Painters
34. Antonello da Messina
35. Flemish and German
    Painters
36. The Bellini family
37. Alvise Vivarini
    and minor painters

from the 15th century
38. Vittore Carpaccio
39. Carpaccio and minor
    painters
40. Lorenzo Lotto
41. Greek Ikon-Painters
42. Majolicas
43. Libreria Manin
44. Servizio Ridolfi

Rooms l–11. Museo
del Risorgimento

Second Floor

The staircase by Room 22 leads to the **Second Floor**: on the right is the **Picture Gallery**, on the left the **Museo Risorgimentale**.

With his passion for history, Teodoro Correr clearly understood the documentary value of paintings.

During the years of the late 18th and early 19th century few collectors bothered with the 15th century; so the noble Venetian, though his contemporaries looked at him askance, was able to easily acquire Quattrocento Venetian paintings of remarkable beauty (above all by Giovanni Bellini, Antonello da Messina and Cosmè Tura) and numerous paintings by Pietro Longhi, an 18th century Venetian painter, so completely ignoring market tendencies.

The 18th-century works have been placed in Ca' Rezzonico, while paintings from the primitives to the early 16th century have been installed on the second floor of the Procuratie Nuove; the Museo Correr has one of the largest and most select collections of the latter in the world.

Early Venetian painting has close links with the art of the nearby Eastern Empire, of which Venice formed one boundary and also a link with the West.

Down to the first half of the 13th century, mosaic cycles were one of the most outstanding features of Venetian art. The Basilica of San Marco is a remarkable showcase of these.

The artists who worked in the basilica either came from Byzantium or were generally under the influence of its hieratic art, as also happened in many other Italian towns at that time, including Rome.

Ferrarese/Bolognese painter c. 1490–95, Man with a Red Beret.

Room 24

Room 24 (Veneto-Byzantine painters) contains works in the courtly and refined style of the second half of the 13th century and first half of the 14th.

It was only in about the 1260s that the first frescoes or panel paintings appeared in Venice; previously mosaic was dominant.

In particular, note one of the earliest examples of Venetian panel painting: the sepulchral casket known as the *Cassa "della beata Giuliana" di Collalto,* who died in 1262. It comes from the monastery of Santi Biagio e Cataldo at the Giudecca; its name derives from the depiction, inside the lid, of the Blessed

Juliana kneeling before the saints to whom the monastery was dedicated. The painter's Western

expressiveness—and rejection of the schemes of Byzantine art—are particularly marked.

*Veneto painter from the
mid-13th century,* Chest
of the Blessed Juliana.

*Veneto-Byzantine
painter active in the
mid-14th century,*
Crucifixion with Saints.

Room 25

The glass door leads to **Room 25**, devoted to **Paolo Veneziano and Venetian painters of the 14th century**. Known to have been active between 1333 and 1358 and to have died before September 1362, Paolo is one of the key figures in the emancipation of Venetian painting from Byzantine models. Yet his stylistic development is the reverse of what one might expect. Paolo's earliest work seems more deeply personal and closer to mainland traditions, while the later work is more obedient to the dictates of Eastern art. The paintings in this room date from his later period: the *Six Saints* (Augustine, Peter, John the Baptist, John the Evangelist, Paul and George) is from a polyptych (the central panel is lost) from the parish church of Grisolera, and the very fine *St. John the Baptist*. This is probably a fragment from the Venetian cathedral of San Pietro in Castello, and is a good example of the combination of refined Eastern tradition with Western Gothic. The other 14th-century polyptyches in this room exemplify aspects of Venetian painting in the period: the triptych with folding panels on the left

represents the *Crucifixion, Stories of Christ and the Virgin, Allegorical and Mystical Figures, Prophets and Fathers of the Church*, a "summa" of the figurative repertoire of the period. The two paintings of the *Madonna and Child* and the triptych

with the *Madonna, Pietà* and *Saints* reveal clearly the relationship between art in the Veneto and Greek Dalmatian and Cretan painting. Also of interest is the painting of *St. Peter*, attributed to a painter from the Veneto in the mid-14th century.

Paolo Veneziano,
St. John the Baptist,
fragment of a panel.

Room 26

The work of **Lorenzo
Veneziano (Room 26)** is
documented in Venice between
1356 and 1372. His paintings,
unlike Paolo's, are firmly in the
mainstream of Gothic art then
triumphant in the Po valley.
There are two fine works of his
here: on the left is part of a
larger polyptych with *Figures
and Stories of Saints* and on
the right another panel of
a polytych signed and dated
1369 along one edge; it
represents the *Giving of
the Keys to St. Peter*: the
remaining fragments of this
work are in Berlin. The
Four Saints at the far end
of the room, long attributed
to Lorenzo, is probably by
a follower of his, Jacobello
Bonomo (documented between
1370–1390).

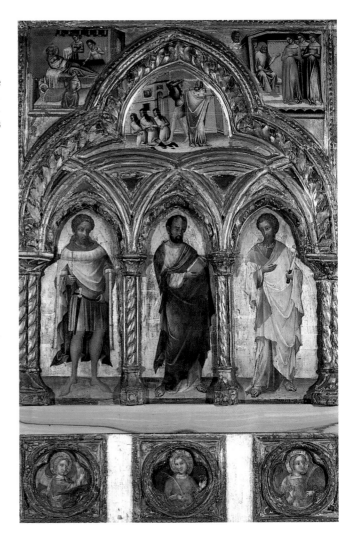

*Lorenzo Veneziano,
polyptych with* Figures
and Stories of Saints.

Room 27

The lacy stonework of the reliefs on certain Venetian palaces mostly date from the period of **Decorated Gothic (Room 27)**, a style that originated in the North of Europe and had a long history in Venice.
The reliefs in Room 27 are from this period. Worthy of note is the statue carved by one of the great masters of the period, Iacobello Dalle Masegne (who also carved the Iconostasis in San Marco): this represents the Doge Antonio Venier kneeling; originally he would also have been holding a standard. Instead of following established official models, the statue is charged with dramatic tension and seems to be a true portrait.
Also of great interest are the fragments of fresco removed from a private house near San Marco and transferred to canvas (on the right-hand and end walls).

Veneto painter of the 14th century, Allegory of the Virtues, *detail of a detached fresco.*

Iacobello Dalle Masegne, Portrait of Doge Antonio Venier Kneeling, *marble.*

Room 28

Room 28 is devoted to **Gothic painting** and arranged in two sections. The first part (Room 28.1) contains works from the late 14th century and early decades of the 15th; the second (Room 28.2) displays paintings by one of the leading 14th-century artists in Venice: Stefano Veneziano, or Stefano di Sant'Agnese, as well as other artists active at the end of the century. The works in the first section include the *Madonna with Child, St. Paul and St. John the Baptist*, recently attributed to a painter of Rimini known as the Maestro dell'Arengo, and a *Crucifix* painted on both sides so that the images could always be visible to the faithful when it was carried in procession. Stefano Veneziano painted the fine *Madonna and Child Enthroned* (first on the left), a work signed dated 1369, and the later *St. Christopher with the Christ Child*, parts of a single polyptych painted for the Scuola dei Forneri at the Madonna dell'Orto, now in the church of San Zaccaria, dated 1385. There is also a *St. Michael* from the bottega of a Paduan master of the period of Guariento, and *Four Saints*, attributed to Jacobello di Bonomo.

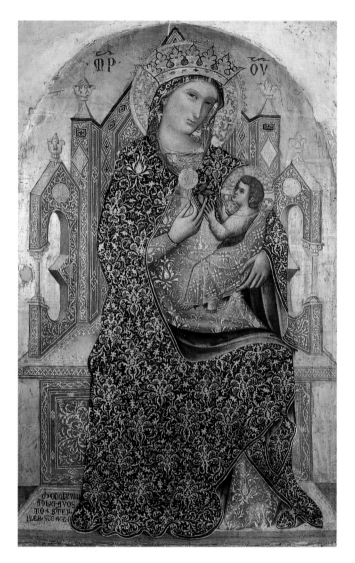

Stefano di Sant'Agnese,
Madonna and Child.

Workshop of Guariento,
The Archangel Michael.

Room 29

The next room, **Room 29**, is divided into two sections: Room 29.1 (**International Gothic: the origins**) and 29.2 (**International Gothic: the protagonists**). They contain masterpieces of the refined Gothic art that spread through the courts of all Europe from the end of the 14th century and all through the 15th. Various cities of the Veneto (especially Venice and Padua) were leading centres of this style. Among the pioneers in the first section are the *Madonna and Child in a Garden*, ascribed to a painter active in Verona in the first half of the Quattrocento, and, the fine panel painted on both sides, with *Angelic Musicians* on the front and *St. Cosma* on the back, probably by a Venetian

painter, largely influenced by Michelino da Besozzo, another leading representative of International Gothic. These are probably the doors of the predella of a polyptych which has been dismembered. Also note the two interesting panels with the *Martyrdom* and *Death of St. Mamete* by Francesco de' Franceschi, a Venetian painter who was active in the mid–15th century and influenced by Antonio Vivarini's style. The second section of this room contains works by two of the major International Gothic artists in Venice: Jacobello del Fiore and Michele Giambino. Jacobello (documented from 1400–1439) was responsible for the very tender *Madonna and Child* bearing the artist's signature and dating from 1420–1430.

The refined elegance of Michele Giambino is evident in the *Madonna and Child with a Goldfinch*. The room also has other paintings by Tuscan masters of this style: the *St. Ermagora and St. Fortunato* by Matteo Giovannetti, an assistant of Simone Martini, and fragments of some chests painted by the anonymous Master of the Jarves chests, decorated with *Stories of Alatiel*.

Jacobello del Fiore,
Madonna and Child.

Follower of Michelino da Besozzo, Choir of Angels.

Francesco de' Franceschi, Martyrdom of St. Mamete.

*Master of the Jarves
chest*, Stories of Alatiel.
*Sala dei Protagonisti del
Gotico Internazionale.*

Room 30

The *Pietà* by the Ferrarese artist **Cosmè Tura** in **Room 30** clearly reveals Teodoro Correr's intelligence as a collector: this work was completely out of favour in the period when it was acquired but it is of fundamental importance in understanding the influences at work on 15th-century painting in the Veneto. It is an original combination of Northern European qualities with motifs from the paintings of Piero della Francesca and the sculptures of Donatello: it can be dated to about 1468. The room also contains a small *Portrait of a Man* attributed to a painter notably influenced by the school of Ferrara.

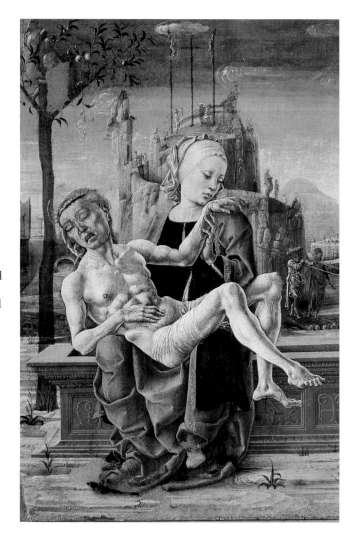

Cosmè Tura, Pietà, *dating from c. 1468.*

Room 31

The room is divided into two sections. The first , **Room 31.1** contains Quattrocento works clearly of Ferrarese origin. Note especially the *Madonna and Child* formerly attributed to Francesco Benaglio, dating from the end of the 15th century. The Madonna clearly reveals the relationship with Central Italian painters, notably Piero della Francesca, an influence widely felt in the art of Ferrara.
The second section, **Room 31.2**, is devoted to the painter Bartolomeo Vivarini of Murano and his pupil Leonardo Boldrini. After training in Padua, Vivarini came under the influence of Andrea Mantegna. On display are two versions of the *Madonna and Child*: the one on the right is signed and can be dated to about 1460. A peculiarity of these two works is the presence at this rather late date of the somewhat old-fashioned gold ground. Leonardo Boldrini, a Venetian and follower of Vivarini, is thought to have painted the *Nativity* and the *Presentation at the Temple* (c. 1475) and the later altar triptych with the *Madonna and Child*, St. Jerome and St. Augustine.

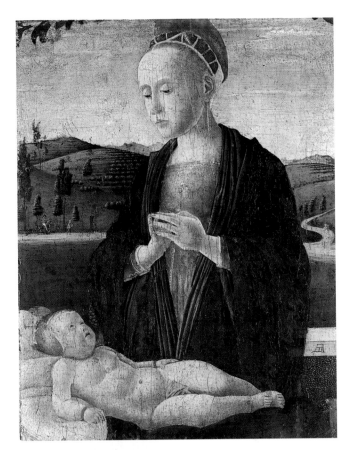

Francesco Benaglio, Madonna and Child.

Leonardo Boldrini, Nativity.

Room 32

Room 32 (Sala delle Quattro Porte) is one of the few chambers in the Procuratie Nuove to retain its original architecture (late 16th–early 17th century). The doorways, now walled up, are 18th-century work. The furnishings go back partly to the 16th and partly the 17th centuries. Apart from the fine woodwork, still well-preserved, note the papier-mâché *Madonna and Child* by Jacopo Sansovino. This late Cinquecento relief used to be in the Corte Scotti in Campo San Luca.

Bartolomeo Vivarini,
Madonna and Child.
Sala delle Quattro Porte.

Jacopo Sansovino,
Madonna and Child,
*papier-mâché. Sala
delle Quattro Porte.*

Room 33

The active cultural links between Venice and the Flemish painters are partly illustrated by the next room, **Room 33 (Flemish painters of the 15th century)**. It contains interesting works like the *Adoration of the Magi* by Pieter Bruegel the Younger and *Christ in Limbo* by a follower of Hieronymus Bosch. Particularly refined are the panels painted on both sides with the *Annunciation* and *Two Saints*.

Pieter Bruegel the Younger, Adoration of the Magi.

Room 34

One of the greatest of all painters is **Antonello da Messina**, known to have been active in Venice in 1475–1476. He is represented in **Room 34** by a masterpiece, the *Pietà with Three Angels*, one of the museum's outstanding acquisitions. The painting is all the more precious as being Antonello's only work still in Venice, where his influence on the artistic tradition was profound. (Among other things, he probably introduced the technique of oil painting, hitherto used only by Flemish artists.) The panel was originally in the Doge's Palace, in the Sala del Consiglio dei Dieci, where Marco Boschini saw it and left a description in the 17th century. The painting is poorly preserved and seems to have lost the lower section; yet its quality is clearly apparent in the best-preserved sections, the landscape and the body of Jesus. It is unusual in that, though it was definitely painted in Venice, it depicts the church of San Francesco in Messina, a tribute by the painter to his native town. The room also has two splendid Flemish works: a *Crucifixion* by **Hugo van der Goes** and a *Madonna and Child* by **Dieric Bouts**, which both reflect the bonds between Antonello da Messina's art and that of Flanders.

Dieric Bouts, Madonna and Child.

Antonella da Messina,
Pietà with Three Angels,
the only work by the
Sicilian painter left
in Venice. Room 34.

Room 35

**Room 35 (Flemish
and German artists
of the 15th and 16th
centuries)** brings together
Flemish and German
paintings, obviously much
in demand in Venice, dating
from the late 15th and early
16th centuries. Note the
Pleasures of the Prodigal Son,
by a painter in the circle of
Paul Coecke , and the
Temptations of St. Antony,
by an artist influenced by
Bosch, perhaps Herri Met
de Bles, nicknamed "Civetta."
There is also a *Portrait
of* a Lady attributed to
Bartholomeus Bruyn
(1493–1555).

Circle of Paul Coecke,
Pleasures of the Prodigal
Son.

*Follower of Bosch
in Antwerp,*
The Temptations
of St. Antony.

Room 36

Room 36 is one of the most significant in the museum and represents one of the peaks of Venetian painting. It contains works from the foremost Quattrocento painter's workshop in Venice, that of the **Bellini** family. Giovanni Bellini, like Antonello, was one of the greatest of Western painters. Teodoro Correr himself possessed three of his finest works: a *Crucifixion*, *The Dead Christ Supported by Two Angels* and a *Transfiguration*. The *Madonna and Child*, here displayed on an easel and commonly known as the Madonna Frizzoni, was donated to the museum in 1919

by Frizzoni, its last owner. These four remarkable paintings belong to Bellini's early period; the *Crucifixion*, probably done in about 1455 is actually one of his very

earliest works and was strongly influenced by his brother-in-law Andrea Mantegna. Jacopo, Giovanni's father, is here represented by a *Crucifixion*, which is part of the predella of which three other panels are in museums in Ferrara and Padua. It may have come from San Zaccaria. This is a work of great expressive power, probably painted in the mid-15th century, at the peak of his career. Gentile Bellini, Giovanni's brother, painted the noteworthy *Portrait of Doge Giovanni Mocenigo*, probably unfinished because of the painter's departure for Constantinople in 1475.

Gentile Bellini,
Portrait of
Doge Giovanni Mocenigo.

Jacopo Bellini,
Crucifixion.

Giovanni Bellini, The
Dead Christ Supported
by Two Angels.

Following pages
Giovanni Bellini,
Transfiguration.

Giovanni Bellini,
Crucifixion.

MISEREMINI·MEI·SALTEM
VOS·AMICI·MEI·

Room 37

Room 37 (Alvise Vivarini and minor artists of the late Quattrocento). Among painters active in the Veneto in the second half of the 14th century, this room exhibits the work of Alvise Vivarini, the heir to a great Muranese workshop, from which comes the *St. Antony* displayed on an easel (the frame is probably original). A *Sacra Conversazione* by Giovanni da Martino da Udine is dated 1498. A work of great beauty, despite its poor state of preservation, is the *Madonna and Child with St. Nicholas and St. Lawrence*, a mature work of Gian Battista Cima da Conegliano dating from the second decade of the16th century. Marco Basaiti may be the author of the fine *Portrait of a Man in a Cap* and Bartolomeo Montagna from Brescia, who painted the *Madonna and Child with St. Joseph*, dating from the early Cinquecento, were both influenced by Alvise Vivarini.

Marco Basaiti,
Portrait of Man in a Cap.

Marco Basaiti, Madonna and Child with Donor.

Bartolomeo Mantegna, Madonna and Child with St. Joseph.

Benedetto Diana, Pietà.

Room 38

Vittore Carpaccio
(c. 1460–1525/26) was one
of the most refined Venetian
painters of the later
Quattrocento. His art
embodies the splendour of
Venetian society in his day and
the Museo Correr has one of
his most celebrated paintings,
Two Venetian Noblewomen,
better known as *The
Courtesans*, the title given
it by Romantic literature
(**Room 38**). This panel, a
fragment of a larger
composition, can be dated
to the first decade of the
Cinquecento and is a work
of the artist's maturity. The
vase on the right side of
the painting bears the arms
of the Priuli family, to which
the women evidently belonged.
Also displayed here is *St. Peter
Martyr*, another late work,
part of a lost polyptych
originally in the Venetian
church of Santa Fosca.

**Two Venetian
Noblewomen**:
noblewomen or
unscrupulous courtesans?
The subject of this
celebrated work by
Carpaccio was much
debated until the recent
identification of a panel
at the Paul Getty
Museum, Malibu, as its
missing upper section. It
depicts a *Hunting Scene*
and sheds light on the
painting's true meaning:
two noblewomen, bored
and wearied, await their
husbands who are intent
on hunting waterfowl on
the lagoon. This
interpretation is
confirmed by many
symbolic details, such as
the women's dresses and
the objects in the
painting, as well as the
arms of the noble Priuli
family on the vase at the
right.

Vittore Carpaccio, Two
Venetian Noblewomen.

Room 39

In 1504 Carpaccio painted the cycle of *Stories of the Virgin* for the Scuola degli Albanesi. One of five paintings depicting the *Visitation* is in **Room 39 (Carpaccio and minor painters of the early Cinquecento)** together with other interesting 16th century Venetian works. A remarkably fine work is the *Portrait of a Gentleman in a Red Cap* (on an easel), by an unknown artist: he seems to have been from Ferrara or Bologna and active at the end of the Quattrocento. Also by an unknown master, but closer to the manner of Bellini, is the *Portrait of a Young Man in a Fur Coat* (also displayed on an easel). Though poorly preserved, the *Circumcision* by Marco Marziale is another admirable work. Also note the *Madonna and Child with St. Peter*, attributed to an artist close to Bissolo.

Marco Marziale,
The Circumcision.

Venetian painter
of the late 15th century,
Portrait of a Young Man
in a Fur Coat.

Room 40–44

The work of Lorenzo Lotto is remarkable in its development. He was an outstanding Venetian artist, mainly active in other parts of Italy. **Room 40 (Lorenzo Lotto and the High Renaissance. Collection of Ivories)** contains a *Madonna and Child* (displayed on an easel) painted in about 1525. Other paintings displayed are by Girolamo and Francesco da Santacroce, who trained in the shadow of Giovanni Bellini. Girolamo is the author of the *Nativity*, while Francesco did the *Vision of St. Jerome* as well as the *Madonna and Child, The Infant St. John the Baptist and Two Angels.* The display-cases contain French and German ivories of the 16th and 17th centuries. **Room 41** contains the work of **Greek Ikon-Painters from the 16th and 17th centuries.** Greek painters, mainly from Crete, were known as *Madonneri*, since their many Venetian workshops mainly turned out ikons for the popular market. The great Doménikos Theotokópoulos (called El Greco) was trained in this school. Two of the paintings here have been compared to his early work; they are the *Last Supper* and *St. Augustine at Prayer.*

The Civic Collections have a rich collection of **majolica,** only part of which is on display in **Room 42,** which contains a selection from the main 16th- and 17th-century schools. The **Manin Library** in **Room 43** comes from the palace of Ludovico Manin, the last of the doges, at San Salvador. The bookcases are late-18th century work, carved in the incipient Neo-Classical style. **Room 44 (Servizio Ridolfi)** contains a china service which probably belonged to Piero Ridolfi, who married a daughter of Lorenzo il

Lorenzo Lotto, Madonna del latte, *dating from c. 1525. Room 40.*

Magnifico. The splendid pieces date from 1515–1520 and were probably the work of a Venetian bottega.
They are decorated with *Stories of Orpheus* taken from Ovid's *Metamorphoses* and the *Hypnerotomachia Poliphili*. The other rooms on the second floor of the museum are now used for temporary exhibitions.

16th-century Graeco-Roman painter, The Wedding at Cana, *Sala dei Madonneri Greci del XVI e XVII secolo. Room 41.*

Orazio Fontana, Carafe decorated with an allegory of Strength, *ceramic. Room 42.*

Museo del Risorgimento e dell'Ottocento Veneziano

This museum is devoted to the history of Venice from the fall of the Republic in 1797 down to its annexation with the unified Kingdom of Italy (1866). It was reorganized in 1980. The Austrians occupied Venice for the first time from 1797 until 1805, the year when Napoleon united the city to the kingdom of Italy. These eight years are the theme of the items in **Rooms 1 and 2**: the first is devoted to Freemasonry, widespread as a secret society in Venice in the later decades of the 18th century. The second period of Austrian rule lasted from 1815 (the Congress of Vienna) to 1848, when Venice was briefly freed by the patriots Daniele Manin and Niccolò Tommaseo; this period is covered by **Room 4**. The last period of Austrian rule stretched from 1849 to 1866; many items from this period are in **Room 8**. Napoleon first entered Venice in November 1807 and the objects in **Room 3** illustrate the actions of the emperor and the varying reactions of the inhabitants. The risings of 1848 and 1849, when Venice rose against the Austrians (like many other Italian towns) are documented in **Rooms 5–6–7**. **Room 9** is devoted to the renowned patriot Daniele Manin.

Ary Sheffer, Portrait of Daniele Manin.

Caffi Ippolito, Night bombing of 24 May 1849 in Marghera.

Karl Zompis, Metternich Fleeing.

Biblioteca Marciana

Also called the **Libreria Sansoviniana** after its designer, Jacopo Sansovino (1536–1588), this building occupies the western side of the Piazzetta di San Marco. One of the richest and most representative of monumental Renaissance buildings in Venice, it was designed to house the great library that Cardinal Bessarione, Patriarch of Constantinople and papal legate to Venice, gave the Serenissima in 1468. Its construction was very complicated: it stands on a site previously occupied by Veneto-Byzantine buildings dating from the 11th–15th centuries. Work started in 1536 but was interrupted in 1545 by the collapse of the vault of an inner chamber, for which disaster Jacopo Sansovino spent some days in prison. Work was resumed soon after but broke off again in 1554, when construction had reached the sixteenth arch. Vincenzo Scamozzi only completed the building in 1583–1588, adding five more arches and partially restructuring the interiors.

Raised three steps above Piazzetta San Marco, the Libreria Sansoviniana consists of two storeys, an arcade at ground level and a loggia above. The arches that run the length of both storeys rest on pillars flanked by semi-columns, with Doric below and Ionic above. In the upper order the arches, together with a balustrade and twinned side columns, frame the tall balconies. Between the two storeys runs an architrave, decorated with metopes and triglyphs in relief, while above there is a trabeation richly carved with *festoons of vegetable forms, putti* and *masks*, a decorative motif suggested by an ancient sarcophagus, which in that period was to be seen in the home of the noble Venetian Grimani family. The balustrade of the attic storey recalls Michelangelo's Palaces on the Capitol in Rome: on it stand pillars with statues of the *Olympian deities* and *heroes elevated to Olympus*. Certain scholars hold that these sculptures form part of a coherent decorative scheme which expresses the Neoplatonic theme of the triumph of the spirit over matter and is developed in the *Mythological stories* in relief on the intrados of the lower arches and the *Victories, Arts,* and *Virtues* under the trabeation of the first storey. Among the principal artists who worked on the deco-

Silver-gilt binding with the Crucifixion and the Resurrection of Christ (detail).

Detail of the attic-balustrade of the Biblioteca Marciana with statues of pagan divinities.

ration under Sansovino were Danese Cattaneo, Pietro da Salò, Bartolomeo Ammannati, Tommaso and Girolamo Lombardi (the last-named executed the frieze on the cornice), while the statues above the balustrade were completed in 1588–1591 by a team of artists that included Tiziano Minio, Lorenzo Rubini and Alessandro Vittoria. The profusion of ornament and the pictorial effect achieved by the alternation of voids and solids create intriguing patterns of light and shade on the front elevation.

Passing through the door flanked by two *Caryatids* by Alessandro Vittoria (1553–1555), we reach the interior of the Library by a *staircase* comprising two flights of steps and covered by barrel vaulting, with cupolas above the landings. It was built in 1553–1559 and is richly decorated with stucco ornaments by Alessandro Vittoria and paintings by Giovanni Battista Franco (first flight) and Battista il Moro (second flight and the first landing). They express man's power to rise above matter (symbolised by the planets and elements) and attain eternity (the figure of *Wisdom* at the top of the staircase) through the exercise of the *Virtues* (depicted in the second flight of steps). After the staircase (notice the Cinquecento *View of Venice* by Jacopo dei Barbari on the first floor) one enters the *Vestibule*, originally designed for lectures on philosophy and classical literature and later altered by Scamozzi to house a collection of antiquities given to Venice in 1587 by the Cardinal and Patriarch of Aquileia Giovanni Grimani. At the centre of the vault, frescoed with architectural designs by Cristoforo and Stefano Rosa (1559–1560) is a canvas of *Divine Wisdom*, painted by Titian, c. 1564. A

Biblioteca Marciana,
also known as the
Libreria Sansoviniana.

Detail of sculptural
decoration of the facade
of the Biblioteca
Marciana depicting
a River God.

Vestibule of the
Biblioteca Marciana
converted to use as a
museum of statuary,
in a drawing by Antonio
Maria Zanetti.

Titian, Wisdom.
Painting at the centre
of the vault in the
vestibule of the
Biblioteca Marciana.

Giovan Battista Zelotti,
Modesty. Vault of the
Salon of the Biblioteca
Marciana.

*Vault of the staircase of
the Biblioteca Marciana
with stucco deocrations
by Alessandro Vittoria.*

doorway, surmounted by an epigraph commemorating the arrival of Cardinal Bessarione's library, leads into spacious *Salone* (about 26 × 10 metres). It has a wooden ceiling with coffers decorated with *grotesque motifs, foliage, cupids* and *harpies* by Giovan Battista Franco and assistants. It contains twenty-one canvases painted between 1556 and 1559 by seven different artists, chosen, according to the records, by Sansovino and Titian. Starting from the entrance, they are: *Nature and the Seasons, Nature with Pallas Athene and Jove, Religion and the Gods*, by Giovanni Mio known as Il Fratina; *Art, Mercury and Neptune, Pallas Athene and Hercules* and *Fortune and Strength* in the next range are by Giuseppe Porta, known as Il Salviati. They are followed by *Agriculture and the Gods, Diana and Acteon*, and *Solicitude, Labour and Exercise* by Giovan Battista Franco and *Vigilance and Patience* and *Glory and Beatitude* by Giulio Licinio; while the tondo of *Sculpture* was refashioned in 1635 by Bernardo Strozzi. Giovan Battista Zelotti painted the *Mathematical Sciences, Goodness* and *Virtue*, and *Modesty*; while Paolo Veronese and Andrea Medulic called Lo Schiavone were responsible respectively for *Song, Music, Honour,* and *Princeliness, Prowess in Arms*, and *Priesthood*. Particularly rich is the decoration of the side walls, adorned in 1562–1572 with canvases of *Philosophers* by various hands. Paolo Veronese did the two beside the portal, Jacopo Tintoretto those on the left wall and probably the end wall, too, while Salviati, Giovan Battista Franco and Lambert Sustris painted the *Philosophers* on the wall towards Piazzetta San Marco.

A display case in the chamber contains two books with precious *bindings*: one silver dat-

Cupola above the first landing on the staircase, with stucco decoration by Alessandro Vittoria and paintings by Battista del Moro.

Reading room of the Biblioteca Marciana.

Following pages
Paolo Caliari known as Veronese, Plato *and* Aristotele. *Salon of the Biblioteca Marciana.*

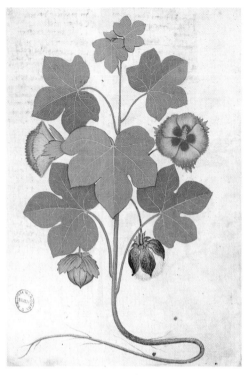

ing from the 14th to the 15th centuries and depicting the *Crucifixion and Resurrection of Christ*, the other silver-gilt from the 13th century, with enamels representing *Christ* (recto) and the *Madonna* (verso) surrounded by Saints.

Exhibits in the Biblioteca Marciana include various bindings of metal, chased or stamped leather, and cloth, important illuminated codices and ancient books. They include *New Testaments* dating to the 9th–11th centuries, the *Psaltery of the Emperor Basil II*, a *Divina Commedia* with miniatures by a Lombard-Veronese artist of the second half of the 14th century, a series of *chansons de geste* with illuminations by Franco-Venetian workshops in the 14th century, the *History of Charlemagne*

Miniature from a 15th-century Herbarium, the Liber de simplicibus.

Deed of gift to the library made by Cardinal Bessarione.

Portrait of Francesco Petrarch, *miniature in a codex of the Biblioteca Marciana.*

with 15th century Persian miniatures, and *De remediis utriusque fortunae*, interesting also as containing a miniature *Portrait of Petrarch*. The most important codex in the library and one of the most representative of the art of illumination, is the *Grimani Breviary*, named after Cardinal Domenico Grimani who donated it to the Republic in 1523. His portrait is in a plaquette mounted in the binding (the verso has a portrait of *Antonio Grimani*). This codex has 831 parchment pages, more than eighty of them illustrated with scenes of *aristocratic life and country pursuits* during the twelve months of the year (a sort of calendar), *Stories from the Old and New Testaments*, the *Mysteries of Religion* and *Stories of Saints*. The artist's identity is debated (Memling, Gerard of Gand, Jan Gossaert, known as Mabuse, Alexander and Simon Bening have all been suggested); it is clear that they were produced by the school of Gand and Bruges in the late 15th or early decades of the 16th century. Also interesting are the Venetian *antiphonaries* and *missals* from the 14th-15th centuries, a copy of Antonio Filarete's *De Architectura* and a 15th-century *Herbarium*. Also noteworthy are the *incunabula* and printed *books* from the 15th-16th centuries, of various provenance (Venice, Ferrara, Florence, Germany and France). In 1907 the *Biblioteca Marciana* was moved to the Palazzo della Zecca; in recent years the Libreria Sansoviniana has been used for exhibitions (for admission ask at the Biblioteca Marciana).

Section devoted to manuscripts and incunabula in the Biblioteca Marciana.

Archaeological Museum

The Archaeological Museum is housed in the Procuratie Nuove. Entry is by a door (no. 17) through an arch of the Sansovinian Library. The Archaeological Museum has an important collection of Greek and Roman sculptures, fragments of architecture, funerary altars, bronzes, statuettes carved in semi-precious stones and ceramics, ivories, epigraphs, Assyro-Babylonian objects and a collection of Roman coins from the 3rd to the 1st century BC. The core of its current holdings is made up of sculptures (in marble, mostly from Rome) from the collection of Cardinal Domenico Grimani, donated to the Venetian Republic in 1523. To this was added, in 1586, the collection of Giovanni Grimani (nephew of Domenico and Patriarch of Aquileia), followed by various bequests, including those by the Contarini, Morosini, Nani, Farsetti, Molin and Zulian families. The collection was originally housed in the Doge's Palace; in 1586 it moved to a chamber in the Libreria Sansovinia, and then returned, in the early 19th century, to its original location. The present premises date from 1923–1926, and since 1939 the museum has also held the archaeological collection of the Museo Civico Correr. In 1996 the arrangement was altered and the labels and other documentary information were fully updated to facilitate eventual production of a scholarly catalogue. Before entering the exhibition rooms the visitor crosses a **court** bounded by an arcading with three orders of architecture: some fragments of architecture are on display here. A stair leads to the loggia on the first floor (**Room I**), with *epigraphs* from the second century BC to the 2nd century AD, *cinerary urns* and *Roman sculptures*. **Room II** holds the *coin collection*, while **Room III** has interesting Roman *statues* after Greek models from before the 5th century BC. **Room IV** contains original Greek statuary from the 5th and 4th centuries BC, some from the Grimani bequest. Note the twin statue of *Caryatids*, the headless statue of *Pallas Athene* from the early 4th century BC, a statue of *Demeter* of the 5th century BC, and the so-called *Abbondanza Grimani*, an Attic *Kore* of the early 5th century BC. **Rooms V** and **VI** have other examples of Greek and Roman statuary from the 5th and 4th centuries BC, including the *Lyceum Apollo*, a bust of *Dionysus*, and *Dionysus and a Satyr* after a Greek work of the age of Praxiteles. In the centre of **Room VI** is the *Grimani Altar*, its sides decorated with *Bacchic scenes* carved by an excellent late Hellenistic artist. **Room VII** contains small sculptures of various origins and, in the showcase, gems, cornelians, cameos and ivories, including the *Zulian cameo* and an interesting panel from a late 10th-century diptych depicting *St. John the Evangelist* and *St. Paul*. Among the most interesting sculptures in **Room VIII** are a statue of *Ulysses* with the characteristic "pilos" on his head, a copy of a

Bust of Dionysos
in Parian marble.
Sculpture from the
Grimani bequest of 1586.

Statuette of Kore
(Abundance) *from the*
Grimani bequest of 1586.